Resurrecting the Muse

Francesca James

Illustrated by Erica Ollesh
Edited by Cathy Silton and Anita Rehker
Cover Art by Carmen Johnson

Resurrecting the Muse

Francesca James

Illustrated by Erica Ollesh
Edited by Cathy Silton and Anita Rehker

Cover Art by Carmen Johnson

Acknowledgements

Birthing this book has been an adventure
surrounded by tremendous learning and much joy.
It has made me more consistently aware that my life is blessed
with many angels who assist me on my journey.

I have overwhelming gratitude for my daughters, Morgan and Carmen. They are my biggest supporters and my greatest reason to continue to expand and grow.

Antoinette Norrell, supported me
through this process from its inception to the final dotted "i" and crossed "t".

Dante James, Judy Etienne, Lauren Casteel and my mother, Ruby Smith
kept me alive allowing this book to come to pass. In many ways I owe you my life.

I thank Walter Barrett for tireless hours spent as my first editor, coach and dear friend. He desired to see the birth of this book because he truly "gets it".

Donna Whittington, I will always appreciate the way in which you
helped me recognize the importance of honoring each step along the way.

Cathy Silton, you are the perfect blend of intuition, wisdom, compassion and skill.

Anita Rehker, you feel my soul and assist It's expression.

Erica Ollesh, your illustrations are a reflection of how amazing you truly are. I cannot thank you enough for this co-creation, which you allowed so unselfishly.

Michael Bernard Beckwith, I thank you for teaching me not to listen to what you say. Rather, to listen to what you listen to. My love for you runs deep.

Dedication

This book is dedicated to my parents
for their demonstration of love and honoring of each other.

As well, to my daughters, Morgan and Carmen and my grandson, Joey
who keep me in wide-eyed wonder and unending joy.

Contents

Foreword by Dante James xi

Introduction xv

The Blueprint 3

Woman, Remember! 17

Our Intuitive Power: The Spirit of Life 29

Our Economic Power: True Wealth 39

Our Inspirational Power: The Breath of Life 49

Our Uplifting Power: Wisdom 59

Our Sexual Power: Oneness 69

Our Co-Creation Power: The Newness of Life 79

Our United Power: Freedom 91

Resurrection 101

Appendix 105

Foreword

In the six years Francesca and I were married, I felt her power as a healer, teacher, mother, wife, lover, and friend. I also felt the power of her anger, her impatience, her disassociation, her desire to always be in control, her selfishness and her lack of compassion. However, if the saying is true that "we teach best what we most need to learn" Resurrecting the Muse is proof that she is not only a teacher and guide, but has also become her own best student.

When we first met, Francesca was juggling the demands of a very stressful corporate work environment, two pre-teen daughters, and me; the new mate, soon-to-be husband. Shortly thereafter, I accepted a position working for the mayor of Denver, which added to the expectations of after-hours events and social functions on top of the stress of everything else. In contrast, she was also a 25 year yoga practitioner/ teacher and spiritual counselor, guiding people along their journey to a healthier lifestyle of eating, praying, journaling, meditating and other modes of self discovery and improvement. I have also practiced yoga (although not so diligently) in addition to having over 35 years of martial arts training. In that realm, I have had the blessing of being able to train with some amazing teachers, in this country and abroad, and believe I can recognize a caring and gifted teacher. Francesca is a caring and gifted teacher, and I learned much from her in the realm of the Divine.

Then the teacher got sick. The teacher got uterine cancer. There is no question that the illness was a result of her stressful lifestyle, and inability to maintain balance in her life. As I watched her and joined her in fighting her cancer, she was adamant that maintaining who she was as a woman meant keeping her womb intact. From healer to healer we went, all the while being monitored by western medicine and told by most that her uterus was no longer a necessary part of her. She refused to believe that, and felt that to lose her uterus was to lose her power. As the cancer progressed, she became weaker and so did our relationship. I was male, I didn't understand. I was allowed to help in a physical, but not emotional way. We grew apart even as we spent more time together trying to heal her body.

I vividly remember the night when I heard her call my name, and heard her fall to the floor. She was unconscious, and was hemorrhaging badly. As I carried her to the bathtub to clean her, and as we went to the emergency room, I knew the decision to have surgery had been made for her. She has been on her new path ever since. Our marriage did not survive, but we have made the full circle back to friendship. I now see her living out her passion. She has realized that her power was always within her spirit and no surgery can diminish that. She has always been one to seek the Divine, to seek to create her goodness. After the surgery, her power and connection to the Divine Goddess became even stronger. I see her now truly living her path, and following her calling to share the way. I have attended her workshops on relationships and felt her gift. She and I have had heartfelt discussions about why our marriage did not survive. We have taken ownership of our failings and the pain we caused each other. We hugged, blessed what was, and said thank you. We now talk, we laugh, and I hear her Muse at work.

Francesca is passionate about who women are and the power they have, over themselves and in the world. She is passionate about sharing the wisdom of her life, its failings, its triumphs and its messages. She can do no less than present the gift of the Divine because she is connected to its universal power. If you are searching for your balance, if you are feeling like there is something missing in your understanding of "why" or "how", if you are a woman in search of your power, Resurrecting the Muse is your book. Resurrecting the Muse will guide you to your intuitive power and connection; guide you to the wisdom of improving relationships. The practices at the end of each chapter and the journaling are Francesca's gifts to you. As she guides you, through this book, you will come to see your strength within. You will come to see your true connection to the Divine Feminine.

I feel honored to have been asked to write this foreword, and I know not only Francesca's words, but also her spirit, will come through to touch you. If you are holding this book, it is because it is predestined for you. Enjoy the blessings within.

Dante J. James, Esq

Introduction

"Congratulations, Mrs. James. You are my most remarkable recovery ever! Stage III, Level C endometrial cancer...I didn't believe you were going to make it."

I am filled with renewed fascination each time these words of my oncologist cross my mind. My gynecologist concurred. They both actually thought I was going to die, but that thought never crossed my mind. I felt certain I was undergoing an ordeal; garnering an experience from which I would one day have wisdom to benefit myself and others. I heard my inner voice while in the emergency room. It spoke to me from deep within, keeping me afloat as I resisted the strong call to close my eyes and just let go. "This is merely an experience from which you will teach. Your presence and your voice are needed." I heard it clearly. I trusted those words and took them as my Truth. The highest part of me was running this show providing reconnection with the intuitive voice with which I had lost touch. What a dramatic way to regain my alignment, but I was willing to go along for the ride. I completely gave up the need to be in control. The person, who awakened after passing out from hemorrhaging, was not the same person who went thump in the middle of the night. As I returned from unconsciousness lying on the floor in my own vomit, feces and urine with my body convulsing I was instantly aware something had changed in me. I couldn't explain it and didn't talk about it, but I became an observer of my life. I looked in the eyes of fear, worry, love, sadness and some-times anger in the flurry of activity all around me. I was at the center knowing that a new life was being birthed. I had no idea what the process would be or who I would become on the other side, but I knew that dying to the old way of existence was perfect and that whoever would emerge as me would have much to share.

At work I had been a high achiever seeking approval from outside of myself. The fast-paced world of advertising found me very driven, successful and exhaust-ed. Shepherd Hoodwin writes in "Male/Female Energy Ratio" that "male energy is directed, focused, goal-oriented, productive, and outward-thrusting…it corre-sponds with linear, left-brained thinking and with doing." That certainly describes my primary way of existence in the world prior to my resurrection. In my family I focused on everyone's needs but my own attempting to be a good wife and moth-er. I ignored the urging from my inner voice to include me. Hoodwin goes on to say, "Female energy is creative, process-oriented, unstructured, and inward-draw-ing…It corresponds with circular, right-brained thinking, and with being." [1] In my quest for success and acceptance I had lost sight of the feminine aspect, although, I knew that she remained present within me. I had become altogether too familiar with my masculine self even when I thought I was being all woman. I found myself caught in a belief in which my value was determined by outward achievements and approval. I allowed myself to live full force from that belief. I was completely out of balance. Women in our society are exhausted trying to keep up with the demands of their lives while fitting into a world in which we often feel disconnected from our Truth. We are pulled away from our inner guidance and inward process seeking approval from outside of ourselves. The Divine Feminine spoke to me clearly. She

1 Hoodwin, Shepherd, *Male/Female Energy Ratio.* Retrieved March 5, 2008 from
   http://www.michaelteachings.com/m-f_ratio.html

is asking women to let go of the programming which has caused us to forget our innate nature which is intuitive, creative, nurturing and compassionate. She is asking us to remember our inner muse, the place from which we receive our wisdom and inspiration so that we may take pleasure in sharing from it in our interactions with others, assisting them in finding it within themselves.

Many times I have thanked my uterus for being a willing sacrifice for the benefit of my whole being. I have returned to hearing the strong guidance under which I am intended to live and I fully see the magnificence and sacredness of being woman, even though, this book is not intended to be a comparison of men and women. There is no attempt to define one as better than the other. It is meant to be an acknowledgement of the beauty of a world in balance where masculine and feminine energy are recognized and honored. There is a difference in the essential nature of humankind dependent upon whether or not the incarnation is in male or female form. The focus of this book is the essential nature of woman for the purpose of resurrecting her to her rightful place of glory because the world is missing its muse. All of human life comes through her loins by a process which is completely intuitive. There is no intellect or ego involved in the creation of humankind. There is, however, an Intelligence which knows how to create a placenta to nourish the impending being. It beats the heart and draws breath without the need for figuring out or reasoning how. It is evident woman is born wired for intuitive process because intuitive process occurs inside of her body. Science can not create billions of human incarnations each with its own unique fingerprints. Something beyond science, intellect and ego knows how to recreate humankind. It chose your mother as a vessel for co-creation and produced you, an individual expression. Although, there is reference in this book to fertilization, gestation and labor as the blueprint for the way in which human life operates at its finest, it does not mean that carrying out this creative process is a requirement for living a life led by Source. As we remember that each human being walking on planet earth is here because of being birthed through a woman we are reminded that the body "temple" of Woman is indeed sacred. It does not matter whether she makes the decision to allow human rebirth. Her wiring is intact. She has a womb, physically and energetically. From her womb dreams reside and spring forth new life. Woman connects with an inner awareness which once was relied upon by society to guide the way. Yet, we have been programmed to forget the significance of our prior role. Remembering is required for moving forward in empowerment.

Woman stepped into the shadow of man and has dwelled there for generations. Society has endured the challenge of living in a world overflowing with male energy and has lost connection with the intuitive voice. Visionary Michael Bernard Beckwith explains, "We are living in a time in history where a shift has occurred in a major way…It's been this whole masculine way of being in the world that has caused a lot of the problems on the planet: the raping of the earth, the pollution, the wars, the rumors of wars, the whole acquisition consciousness of hoarding and getting and domination, manipulation and control"[2] Now we must find balance in order to allow a more peaceful, harmonious energy into our world. This balance is found in the rebalancing of woman. Rebalancing comes through woman lov-ing herself and forgiving the past. The reemergence of woman knowing, owning, honoring and living from the empowerment of her essential nature brings an un-derstanding that woman carries sacred medicine within her cells which heals our world. In all forms of belief something "sacred" is worthy of respect and honor. The internal, intuitive part of our being is indeed the sacred part. When Woman

---

2 Embracing the Feminine, "Spiritual Liberation-Fulfilling Your Soul's Potential, DVD, directed by Mikki Willis, (Los Angeles: Elevate Films, 2009).

is whole, standing in her power, she can be healed. When Woman is healed everything around her can experience the feeling of healing because woman is that significant. She represents home. All of human life begins by being fed through and by woman. Everyone turns to woman for comfort and nurturance. She uplifts everyone when she is uplifted providing a space for healing to occur. Medicine is imparted from her intuitive, wise inner muse.

I awakened to my authentic self through a path which I would never have chosen, although, I consider it to be one of the greatest gifts of my life. *Resurrecting The Muse* is birthed from my experiences and intuitive insights. I spent many years in Corporate America living outside of my innate self. I lost sight of my needs within the dynamics of my family life. I offer my Truth for others to take into their intuitive nature and decide if it rings true for them as well because I believe the Divine Feminine aspect within is calling us into awareness of our essential, intuitive nature. *Resurrecting The Muse* assists in the remembering and provides a guide for stepping back into authenticity, where we will find balance.

In Classical Mythology we hear of various goddesses who presided over particular art…meditation, memory, music, poetry, etc. They are referred to as Muse. In modern society the Muse is considered one who inspires a poet or artist. In truth, all women are designed to be the Muse because all of humankind begins within her womb and looks to her to inspire and motivate their lives. Unfortunately, the overwhelming feeling of woman's life has caused her to forget this important role and sometimes experience it as burdensome. I certainly did in my past.

When we relate to each other through our inner sense of imbalance we stand the chance of igniting that imbalance which exists in those with whom we are relating. If we can remember when feeling off balance, upset, fearful, or angry to stop and breathe consciously, we can bring balance to ourselves and provide it to those around us. Then when we speak we are in a greater alignment within which spills over to the without. At that point the words come from guidance rather than from the painful memories that have been ignited. We can allow the memories to come up and release rather than imposing them on others. We reunite with the feminine's soft energy and remember the attributes of that energy which gives support and motivation rather than tearing apart.

When woman finds peaceful softness within she will no longer find frustration in giving to others. Sometimes when she doesn't feel like giving of her sustenance she remembers that it is her nature and that her contribution is necessary for the higher good. She will understand and respect the difference in the expression of masculine and feminine energy without unfounded expectations of masculine behaving and processing the same as feminine. She will remember to bring her open hearted gentleness to man knowing that speaking from there inspires him to his further greatness. She will know that at times her communication is more effective with her mouth quiet and her intuitive voice on blast. This is the manner in which woman resurrects the muse.

Harmony and balance is experienced when we follow the inner guidance which is always speaking to us, moving and prodding us toward a more evolved state of being. Yet, we all have old beliefs and memories that replay simply because we've allowed past experiences to be part of our present moments and accepted someone else's beliefs as our truth when, in fact, our Truth only exists within our individual being, heard through that inner voice. No one can tell you your Truth; no one, not even the most gifted intuitive guru… certainly, not me. I encourage you to remember that you have intuition and your intuitive voice is longing to speak through you as kindness, love and compassion.

I speak to you of my Truth because it is what I hear within my being...the words that are whispered to me from within. I believe that we can understand everything about the manner in which human life operates by looking at the way that human existence begins. Since Creative Intelligence gave woman a womb through which she recreates human life it indicates to me that the womb houses new life; not only of humankind, but the newness provided as we manifest our dreams. We hold our dreams and desires within the womb allowing them to grow being nurtured, fed daily from love. We whisper sweetness into them even before we can see them here, in the physical; in time—Its time, not ours—they are born into physical manifestation. We remain aligned to them forever. They require our continued unconditional love, nurturance, motivation and inspiration in order to embrace their ever-expanding potential.

The incarnation of the Divine Feminine aspect into female form is to be revered. Woman is the nurturer of all human life. She is the vessel through whom co-creation with the Creator takes place. She offers her medicine as inspiration and motivation to all when she is connected with her essential nature. Genetic coding uses her womb and her emotions causing her to give birth to newness. Fertilization, gestation, labor and birth are symbolic of how newness emerges. Woman is the personification of this creative process. Woman is the Muse, indisputably powerful. Our society knows it and depends on it. It is time that woman recognizes and depends on it too.

RESURRECTING THE MUSE is intended to help you to remember that you have an intuitive voice, which is intended to be your guidance system regardless of the tug from the outside world. Reunite with it and speak from it. Let it guide and direct your life because the world needs your inspiration. The world needs you to *Resurrect The Muse!*

Resurrecting the Muse

Following every chapter you will find a practice. Each practice serves as a tool to be used for discovering a greater alignment with your inner muse.

Tools for resurrecting the muse: Through commitment to the practice you will gain a sense of empowerment and greater insight. Each practice outlined is to be utilized for a period of seven days before moving on to the next, although, they are practices that you might choose to continue to utilize through out your life. You will need the use of a journal and the commitment to carve out time for you. You know you deserve it!

What I want all women to know is that
within their biology they have the code for enhancing all of life.
The egg can take a sperm and heal the genetics of a defective sperm.
Every time a woman is in her power she upgrades everyone and everything around her.
When a woman is doing better and she's healthier and happier she raises me up.
Whenever a woman gets healthy and happier she heals the earth.
The woman's body is a reflection of the earth and everything we do to take care
of ourselves, to feel pleasure, to be orgasmicly joyous heals the entire planet.

~ Christiane Northrup, MD

CHAPTER ONE

The Blueprint

The way in which human life begins is a blueprint for the way in which human life operates at its finest!

"Much like guided missiles that sense the heat of a plane's engine, sperm are guided to the fertilization site by temperature...the egg 'calls upon' the mature sperm...Apparently, the sperm are guided by temperature when they travel through most of the fallopian tube and navigate by tuning in to the egg's chemical call when they get close to the fertilization site."[1] The egg (feminine energy) calls the sperm (masculine energy) into her embrace. Pure masculine energy meets pure feminine energy. She has drawn him in, guiding the way until at last; aware that he is in her presence he becomes nothing. She becomes nothing. In an instant,

1 Weizmann Institute (2003, February 3). Sperm Use Heat Sensors To Find The Egg; Weizmann Institute Research Contributes To Understanding Of Human Fertilization. *Science Daily*. Retrieved July 1, 2008, from http://www.sciencedaily.com /releases/2003/02/030203071703.ht

both are absorbed into that nothingness to become everything as a third whole-ness is created from their union. Woman is the embodiment of feminine energy. Man is the embodiment of masculine energy. It is in the DNA of woman to *attract* masculine energy into her inner being. It is in the DNA of man to pursue feminine energy with every breath of his being.

    We have a blueprint, which was given to humanity by the creator of life. The blueprint is shown to us unmistakably through the process of human re-creation. In the fertilization process the egg demonstrates the feminine aspect of which woman is an embodiment. The egg is present not seeking after anything. It is in "being" mode. The sperm cells, the doers, begin as a cast of millions competing in a battle to the finish. Man is the embodiment of the "doing" mode of life. Man and woman are representatives of the aspect, which they embody. In their essential nature women conjure, men execute. Clearly; the sperm cell could not reach the final desti-nation without the guidance of feminine energy. Two wholes unite to create a third whole which is potentially feminine and masculine energy in balance. The being and doing aspects come together and represent balance. On the sperm cell's journey, at times, it rests and retunes to the call of the egg which guides the where, when and how of the journey. This is the manner in which rebirth occurs. We have a blueprint for our ever-evolving lives. Humankind is in a continuous state of transformation and rebirth. When we are not in worry, fear, anxiety or concern we are able to be in alignment with our nature and attract our desires. Our intellectual and egoic views, which are the place where fear and worry live, are able to be balanced by the soft, harmonious knowing of the feminine. We take the steps that are shown to us by our intuitive insights. The union of masculine and feminine energy denotes bal-ance. Moving in balance is the way in which we experience the ease and harmony of life. Recognition of the feminine energy has been missing from this equation in our society far too long. The blueprint indicates that woman is intended to stand in her intuitive nature guiding and directing from her knowing, not being led by her masculine intellect and ego. Man, whose basic instinct is to provide, fix, protect, hunt and gather; when in his essential nature; knows that woman's compassionate, nurturing manner is the heaven to his earth. The incarnation of the divine feminine aspect into female form is to be revered. Woman is the motivational muse. When humanity realigns with this Truth and allows the nature of woman to again be honored and respected we will find the balance and harmony intended in life.

There was a time in history when woman was valued for her mystical, life-giving power. Society was centered on woman. She raised the children, made decisions for her community, created art, communicated with the plants to know their healing power. She was partner with man, each honoring, respecting and supporting their respective roles recognizing the importance of each. The culture changed over time. "Laws were introduced, taking rights of inheritance away from woman. Control over her property, finances, and legal affairs was given to men related to her. Her political and social autonomy was taken, and in some places she was considered property."[2] Masculine energy became dominant. The divine feminine energy was dismissed, but it never disappeared. Divine feminine energy lives in the core of all. She is love, honesty, compassion, creativity and she is the energy through which new life emerges. While the role of woman in society is relatively the same as it was in the past, that role is no longer honored and respected because woman has lost sight of its importance. Somewhere along the way the competitive nature of the masculine energy felt challenged by the attracting nature of the feminine. Woman's character was ridiculed. Woman was told (and she accepted) that

2 Judith Duerk, Circle of Stones: Woman's Journey to Herself (Novato, CA: New World Library, 2004)35.

she is not good enough and her nature became suppressed. Evidently, man began to feel inadequate in comparison to woman. This feeling of inadequacy is rebirthed into the mental atmosphere along with woman's feelings of invalidation; becoming part of the experience of being human.

During my eight-year stint in Catholic School, the idea that humankind is born with original sin was reinforced, over and over again. We learned that Adam and Eve could commune with God in the absolute Utopia known as the Garden of Eden, and had all the magnificence of life at their beck and call in this heaven on earth. They were told they could have *everything* except the fruit from one tree; the tree of knowledge of good and evil, but Eve was disobedient and had no self-control. Eve (Woman) gave into the devil's temptation and seduced Adam (Man) to eat the forbidden fruit, which caused the two of them to be banished from this utopian place. The disobedience to God demonstrated by eating of the proverbial apple is what became known as man's original sin. We were told that, subsequently, each and every human being born needs to be baptized to be cleansed from the stain of this sin that was passed on by Eve's indiscretion. Wow, that's a lot of blame to put on Woman!!! I dismissed the theory of original sin. It was hard for me to accept the common view of babies and children as innocent, pure beings coexistent with being sinful beings. Then recently one day out of the blue, without having a conscious thought about it, I heard from within my being, *"There really is original sin!!!"*

My *aha!* moment came to me because through years of engagement in spiritual counseling I wondered repeatedly why *every* client carries beliefs from childhood that are not Truth-based. There is a common belief in not good enough, should look or behave differently, or need to possess more illusive somethings. The whisper, *"There really is original sin,"* provided my answer. I recognize as true what Ernest Holmes teaches, "...each individual carries around with him (and has written into his mentality) many impressions which he never consciously thought of or experienced... There is a tendency, on the part of all of us, to reproduce the accumulated subjective experiences of the human race."[3] Some call this tendency race consciousness or collective consciousness. I call it collective unconsciousness because it demonstrates that we are out of alignment with pure consciousness; our inborn, intuitive nature. We are walking around unconsciously following and believing opinions, thoughts and experiences of others without determining our own. At birth we are immersed into a human race vibration of memories and beliefs of our families and society, which we allow to become our defining truth. "Sin" is the loss of conscious awareness of the innocence and perfection with which we are born. Existing in that collective unconsciousness in our society is the belief that is told again and again, Woman should not possess too much power. She is the seductress who caused man to be banished from Utopia. If there is truth in the philosophy laid out by Ernest Holmes and countless others that beliefs, experiences, judgments and attitudes of humanity exist in an atmosphere of prevailing thought form and that we tap into and take ownership without even realizing, we are taking on beliefs that are not necessarily our own. We do it without realizing it. We have an inner gauge, but we don't even realize that we aren't paying attention to it. We turn down the volume, but it is never turned off.

There is no right or wrong to our history. However, as we evolve to a new vibration, there is a universal feeling which places humanity in a more loving, compassionate energetic. This energetic is the nature of the Divine Feminine, made flesh as woman. The prevailing belief that floats in the ether blaming Eve for "original sin" is part of the underlying cause of society's dismissal of woman's true

---

3 Ernest Holmes, The Science of Mind (New York, NY: G.P. Putnam's Sons, 1938) 348-349.

nature. The belief that woman caused everyone to be stained with "sin" is at the core of our society promoting woman's "I'm not good enough" thinking. Unconscious beliefs, taken for granted without being questioned, control our behavior in our culture driven by power and the need to control. We need to be baptized by the Muse!

It is taught that baptism is the required method through which we cleanse from sin readying us to go to heaven. Perhaps it is the opposite; when we go to *heaven* we are cleansed. Going to heaven is realigning with our awareness of the magnificent Source from which we are birthed. We are in heaven, the Utopia of the Garden of Eden, when we consciously remember we are worthy because we are made in the image and likeness of worthiness. That which creates life is perfect. We are the reflection of It in the world. We are called back to this "remembering" of the love, compassion, and creative existence: the Divine Feminine aspect, which is our birthright.

The blueprint of life's design is further demonstrated in the birthing process in which woman is the key component. All of human life begins through an intuitive, nurturing process in the home provided by the womb of woman. Yet, woman doubts her own knowing. Inside woman's body, a union of male and female energy occurs, cells divide, organs are formed and breath, the indicator of life, takes place. All the science in the world cannot duplicate the incarnation which occurred inside the womb of your mother. Apparently, what we call the Creator has chosen the body of woman as the center of intuitive creation.

In the gestation phase of co-creation, Woman participates as a witness to what is happening within her being. Human intellect is not in charge. She does not decide how long the gestation process will be. She can't determine the look of the emerging being, whether it will be male or female. No matter how strong the desire to control, woman has no control. She must surrender to the plan of the Divine Feminine which is guiding this movement. All the adjustments needed occur without human intervention. A mucous plug forms, protecting the new life. A placenta is formed for its nourishment. The ligaments soften, the pelvis expands, and the water breaks, all to assist the birth. Something takes over, has Its way and knows what It is doing. The role woman plays is to listen within to know what is required of her...those incessant cravings, the unavoidable need to rest, etc. We are all birthed through an intuitive process, which occurs within the womb of woman and requires her simply to allow intuition to be at the helm of the process that is the blueprint available for reference as we navigate through the adventure of life. When aligned with her inner knowing woman is the navigator through life. Woman is the Muse.

In order to birth new life, woman moves into a time of labor, a significant part of the blueprint. Woman's womb begins to contract indicating that it has become too small a container for the emerging being. Labor is an experience of intense pressure perceived as pain. This intensity is felt not only by the mother but also by the emerging child. Labor brings with it the feeling of "pain," the purpose of which is to clearly secure the attention of the one in pain and let her know that it is time to let go of anything outside, move into a conscious place of alignment with what is occurring, breathing consciously and in synchronicity with what's taking place to acquire a sense of calm. When she lets go of the need to control (because she has absolutely no control) she can experience an elevated state where only the ebb and flow of intense energy experienced as pain remains. Enduring this intense pain just for a while brings to her the tremendous gift of life that she has called forth. She does not know how long the pain will endure, but she has a tool...the breath. Conscious breathing is available to place her in the flow of new life. The breath keeps her in the now moment allowing her mind to be still. On the other hand, when woman is not in alignment with what is going on, when she is in her thinking self desiring to have some control over the process, she tends to experience suffering as her reality. When she is not willing to surrender to the occurrence she will suffer. When the feeling of suffering exists often the woman will seek something to eliminate it. "Research suggests that completely eliminating pain during birth can prolong labor, cause stress to the mother and baby, and increase the likelihood of cesarean surgery. Women, who learn ways to work with pain, rather than eliminate it, increase their chances of having a complication-free, highly satisfying birth." [4] When the woman makes a decision to use outside methods to reduce the pain of labor, it is generally because she has been programmed by someone else's experience to believe that birthing is a fearful, excruciating experience. Giving birth is a natural, normal state for woman. She has been doing it for generations.

Isn't this the way that we are to approach all ventures in our lives? Let go of programming, allow support, breathe, and surrender. Aah, the blueprint! In its proper time and in its own way, the new creation emerges. What is no longer needed is eliminated. The pain subsides, euphoria sets in, mother and child rest. Yet, humankind is forever seeking a way out of suffering. We tend to experience situations which appear opposite from our desires or our expectation as painful. When we recognize that money is not available to meet an obligation, a loved one decides they no longer desire to participate in relationship with us, even small things like driving down a familiar street and encountering a road block when we are in a hurry and concerned about being on time, we lose our sense of balance and forget that we are empowered from within. When faced with unexpected

---

4 Dress, Kara,
Have No Fear When Labor Is Near! Preparation, Their Fear of Childbirth, retrieved January 31, 2009 from http://www.lamaze.org/

situations we have the choice to remain attached to our desired outcome and fight for life to out picture accordingly or we can breathe with the labor pains and allow new birth, welcoming it with joy and amazement as we do a newborn child. The initial feeling of pain is an indication of a change in course, just as in the onset of labor. The attachment to the expected course of action causes the prolonged feeling of pain which becomes suffering. Using the process of birth as the blueprint for the human experience, we can remember that when painful situations occur, they present the opportunity to give birth to our desires and our dreams. It is beneficial in those times of forgetfulness to have someone who remembers to act as your motivation, facilitating your realignment with harmony.

Let me bring it home for you: We are not here on planet earth without a road map indicating which direction to go to enjoy this adventure called life. There is an Intelligence which lives as plant life, the animal kingdom and humankind. It is evident when we see the beauty of a flower in all of its magnificence that perfection simply is. There is no need to seek after it. The flower does not worry whether or not it will receive enough sun, water and love to thrive. It doesn't concern itself with the changing of the seasons. It simply exemplifies beauty, reflecting the perfect nature of its Creator. The same ease and freedom of existence is the potential for every man, woman and child. Our nature, at the core of our being, is identical with the nature of that which creates life. Humankind, just as all expressions of nature exists to reveal the beauty, freedom and perfection of that Creative Intelligence. The Creator has provided guidance. Humankind has been given a blueprint indicating that feminine energy is what guides the direction for anything that is being birthed. Man and woman are both feminine and masculine at the core, but woman is the representation of the feminine while man is the representation of the masculine. The two energies work in conjunction with each other with feminine energy as the guidance system. In all endeavors the feminine aspect must be present to allow the ease of the rebirthing adventure to be present. Otherwise, there is imbalance which allows suffering to occur as we attempt to control. If we remember to follow this blueprint, which is lead by listening to the intuitive call, we aren't caught up in beliefs which are not our own. Rather, we allow two energies to unite creating a third wholeness. There is no room in rebalancing and rebirth for society's mimicking the intuitive nature of woman or dismissal of her invaluable role. The resurrected muse will whisper your Truth into your heart.

Resurrecting the Muse

Take just a few moments to close your eyes and feel the sense of peace that always lives inside of you. Take some conscious, full breaths. Ask your inner muse to reveal herself to you.

With paper on your lap or on a table in front of you and pen in your *non-dominant* hand (the opposite hand from the one with which you normally write) begin to write whatever comes to mind.

It doesn't matter if it makes sense to you or if you make grammatical errors or write in incomplete sentences. You are asking YOUR inner muse to tell you who she is and how she makes herself available to you. You will connect with a feeling within that can be brought forward to live in the outer world.

Do this exercise over the next 7 days. Allow time for completion as you connect with the inspired, motivated, intuitive part of you. Save your writings in your journal.

"Mother, I have learned that every living thing has a heart filled with love, desires, dreams, plans, and great Medicine...the twinkle reflected in the eyes of any Child of Earth mirrors the hidden fire of wisdom that dwells within."

~ Jamie Sams
"The 13 Original Clan Mothers"

CHAPTER TWO

Woman, Remember!

I was raised by a beautiful African-American woman who epitomized June Cleaver, Harriet Nelson and Donna Reed all wrapped up in one well-dressed package. I grew up believing women were never to raise their voices in an unladylike fashion. Their duties were to starch and iron bed sheets and boxers, cook and clean house; and time it perfectly to be ready to greet their husbands returning from work while wearing pearls, high heels and perfectly manicured nails. My father was the bread-winner. My mother was the stunning beauty *behind* the man.

Women were portrayed by the television media as fragile, naïve objects to be seen, though not possessing the intelligence to be heard. No wonder Helen Reddy sang out in 1972, "I Am Woman, Hear Me Roar!!!" I had no idea growing up that inside of woman's genetic coding was the power to heal all of human life; it was a long, laborious road to that understanding for me. However, I can look back and know full well that inside of me the Truth was always speaking, seeking my attention.

Born into a male-oriented world shaped to suit man's needs, our innate womanly empowerment has been twisted to serve others. As women, we typically lose touch with ourselves, live formularized lives unaware of our own uniqueness and the power that resides within, while that power is bottled and often exploited.

Our intuitive power is valued by others, yet we second guess and question our own connection to the Spirit that is Life. I ask women if they are intuitive and they usually answer, "Yes, but..." and then minimize, belittle, or criticize themselves to soften the "Yes." I ask men if women are intuitive and they answer without hesitation, "Of course—and we need them to be." Woman, what are you pretending not to know? *We possess unmistakable intuitive power, and always have!*

Our economic power is harnessed to accumulate image-based toys while our inner lives become more impoverished. Women aren't conscious of how empowered we are. Ironically, in the corporate world, where I worked for many years, woman's power was completely understood and utilized. Seldom did advertising campaigns identify men as their primary target. Women influence and/or make most purchasing decisions. *We possess real economic power, and always have.*

Our inspirational power is on demand 24/7 leaving us panting and out of breath. Although women have entered the public domain of business and politics, arenas off limits to our female ancestors, from decorating to scheduling to coordinating the lives of the children and elder parents, they continue to make most of the decisions in the home. Most of us are exhausted from this dual set of responsibilities and the energy necessary to keep it all in order, yet we do it. *We possess real inspirational power, and always have.*

Our uplifting power is parceled out as needed yet our inner lives are confused and disoriented. During my first interview in advertising, the manager admitted he particularly wanted to hire a woman. His reasons: women are better at multitasking and the presence of women on sales teams always raises the bar, encouraging men to shift into higher gear to keep up the pace, creating a more effective team. *We possess real uplifting power, and always have.*

Our sexual power is used to service others while we feel divided, fragmented, and disconnected within ourselves. Man continues to be possessed by the body of Woman. His sexual antics are the stuff of novels and movies. We all have watched the heads of countless male co-workers, friends and partners turn to view Woman, their imaginations ready to pounce. Even the more mature among the male species seems consumed with their need for connection with the female. *We possess real sexual power, and always have.*

Our co-creation power is necessary for the ongoingness of life yet, fearful of stepping outside the lines drawn for us, we live within imposed boundaries. Women bring forth life. We carry it within for nine months and then thrust it forward in the form of sons and daughters. All human life flows through our wombs, which speaks volumes about the wiring of all women. The signs of life occur there—the heart begins to beat, the brain begins to function, and the embodiment of Spirit is initiated. In the birthing process, woman co-creates with Spirit. *We possess fundamental co-creation power, and always have.*

It is incumbent upon woman to move from the formularized, programmed outwardly focused expression of her empowerment to the essential expression, the sacredness, only found within. It is time to reclaim the power of woman for the sake of our lives, our bodies, our children, our men and our planet. Women are the mothers of all living carrying all that is needed to restore our lives and our world to balanced health. A woman in balance and aware of her empowerment brings all around her into balance and aware of their own power. Woman is the Muse.

During my life in Corporate America I was frequently engaged in conversations with women who proclaimed, "Men want a powerful woman, but when they get one, they don't know what to do with her!" This was my true belief before remembering that woman is innately empowered and attracts to herself a replication of her conscious belief. What I failed to realize, and believe many other women are not recognizing, is the difference between a powerful woman and an empowered one. They are two different species. Our society defines power as "power over." A powerful woman has become the independent woman who can buy her own diamonds and pay her own bills. When woman reaches that stature she believes that she's no match for men. However, typically, that woman (the past life version of me included) is leaning hard on her masculine side. She thinks because she has her hair and her nails done and is wearing her Louboutin shoes that she's *all woman*. Men admire and respect that woman who wheels and deals in the world of business and politics, she inspires his innate competitive nature, but the part of her that immerses into her masculine energy to compete in society is not the aspect of woman that he wants to interact with at home. He is looking for his Muse, the inspiration and motivation for his life. He is seeking the woman who helps to give his life meaning. It is that softer side of woman which appears once she disrobes from her masculine persona. It brings to mind the image of one person sitting on a teeter-totter finding balance only when joined by another. Feminine and masculine energy are intended to operate together. Because woman embodies the feminine an overdependence on her male aspect can bring suffering in her body temple and her relationships. When she allows balance within her being she aligns with her essential self and will find peace there. Remember, when woman is at peace the world can find peace. She wields unparalleled power.

Man desires to love and support woman. It is in his nature to provide and protect. Steve Harvey says, "Encoded in the DNA of the male species is that we are to be the provider and the protector of the family, and everything we do is geared toward ensuring we can make this happen."[1] John Gray tells us, "Men are motivated and empowered when they feel needed."[2] Shaunti Feldhahn writes, "His need to provide weighs him down and he likes it that way. Providing is a primary way to say, 'I love you' "[3] When woman is operating from a closer alignment to masculine nature than from her innate nurturing self, the softness which is needed by our families and our society gets lost. We can function in the world in all the roles which woman plays, but when we lose sight of our essential selves everyone suffers from the imbalance.

David Deida states, "You attract him toward life by your radiance, and give him the energy to endure the crucifixions of life through the power of your love.

Your gifts of energy, of radiance, of attraction, may take the form of your genuine smile, the look of love in your eyes, your touch that enlivens him, anything

---

1 Steve Harvey, <u>Act Like Lady Think Like A Man</u> (New York: HarperCollins, 2009) 15.

2 John Gray, <u>Men Are From Mars, Women Are From Venus: The Classic Guide To Understanding The Opposite Sex </u>(New York: HarperCollins, 1992) 43

3 Shaunti Feldhahn<u>, For Women Only: What You Need To Know About The Inner Lives Of Men </u>(Atlanta: Multnomah, 2004) 75, 80.

that fills his body, mind and emotions with energy, love and life. Then he feels you as his source of delight in an otherwise burdensome world."[4]

Woman is, indeed, multi-faceted. The allowance of all parts of woman is mandatory in an evolved world where she can speak her truth; raised voice or not. In her essential form she is living from a place of inner-guidance which will attract to her all that she needs and all that society is dependent on her to provide. When she remembers to allow the see saw to balance with ease and flow because everyone is connected to woman, they feel her peace.

I once worked as an IBM sales representative. To be an IBMer meant one had to learn the IBM product-line, lingo, attitude, and style of dress. We were sent to employee training regularly to be refinished. These trainings made it clear that female emotion had no place in the corporate environment. Ego was the entryway. Ego was "king" at IBM. I learned the rules for playing in the big leagues with the boys. I learned to play their games, their way. I found myself looking at my environment solely through my eyes without the use of my *vision*. Each time I returned home from IBM training, my significant other noticed my increased edginess and elevated stress level. A conflict raged in my soul, causing great unrest. I didn't quite recognize it or understand its source, but he saw it clearly. The world of Corporate America had no appreciation for my female spirit. It required me to deny essential aspects of myself and to adopt a male persona. The pull for doing it right and being accepted was quite strong. I wanted to be a part of this money-making arena. I wore my colorful dresses under my IBM blazers, but my spirit ached for its True expression. Woman has been stripped of an awareness of the power that resides within her. Our lives are out of balance, our bodies cry out, our spirits ache for their unique expression, and our planet reflects our dis-ease.

---

4 David Deida, It's A Guy Thing: An Owners Manual for Women, Deerfield Beach: (Health Communications, Inc. 1997), 12

Over the years, my awakening to this insightful perspective progressed, but most profoundly and transformatively out of my dis-ease called uterine cancer. All the pretty dresses in the world could not stop the quake inside my womb. Twenty years prior to my illness were spent teaching others how to be healthy. For twelve years I taught yoga with continuing education in nutrition, anatomy, physiology, etc. I ate organic foods, worked out, took all the right steps in my life, yet cancer found its way into my temple. I am clear that this was a cup from which I had to drink. The doctors tried everything possible, detoxifying and prayer worked to show me their power, but the cancer was the potion through which the real healing was to take place. My first of three emergency room trips began the ending of the person I had known myself to be and the birth of an amazing adventure on which I continue.

Just as societies once valued woman's life-giving power, there was a time when most cultures considered a woman's womb sacred. However, before finding Dr. Johnny Johnson, each doctor I consulted -- male and female -- indicated that the uterus is a dispensable part of a woman's anatomy. They claimed the uterus has two purposes -- to grow babies and to grow cancer. They'd say, "It's a parasite! If you don't plan to have more children take it out."

There are still cultures which care for the uterus in a very loving, harmonious and therapeutic manner. Post surgery I had the honor of studying with Mayan midwives in Belize. They say that the uterus is woman's second brain, which thinks, has memories, can inspire dream visions, send messages, and can indicate when to have fear. It is, they believe, woman's direct contact to her spiritual creativity. Repeatedly they claimed that when the uterus is removed, there remains an energetic presence. I believe it to be Truth, thank Goddess. The understanding is that Woman's intuitive nature comes from the interplay of the uterus with the brain, the bloodstream and the hormones. Therefore, when a woman begins to deny her creative expression or allow others to invalidate it, the intuitive flow becomes stagnant and the reproductive organs become diseased. In other words, we live on more planes than just the physical. On an energetic level, female complaints are believed to express a woman's sense of self. Certainly, there are anatomical reasons that the uterus undergoes changes which cause it to have pathological trauma. However, I for one can directly link that pathology with my loss of Self. My doctors were amazed that I had uterine cancer because I did not fit the profile. Yet, inside I knew the answer. At work I had birthed the most successful project of my career. When management realized the significance of the coup, I was told that they were going to take over the expanded version of it and leave me with the crumbs harnessing my economic power for their gain and recognition. What I had created through my passion and my drive the greed and power of the masculine corporate world tried to claim as its own. I was pushed and set aside. I was kicked in the seat of my creativity. They reflected to me the voice in my head telling me that I was not enough. It was the image, after all, with which I had grown up. I did not remember to remember that I am an empowered woman who can attract to herself anything that she desires. I allowed my Light to be dimmed. Soon the hemorrhaging began.

In various cultures, rather than insult womanhood and deny the importance of her reproductive organs, health care practitioners work in conjunction with na-ture intuitively honoring, loving, respecting, and nurturing her natural rhythm. They maintain the health of the female reproductive system because they know the value of woman. Human life cannot continue without her. They acknowledge that our bodies are self-healing, self-regulating, and self-regenerating. The body sim-ply needs our assistance sometimes in removing the obstructions to healing while allowing nature to take care of the rest. This assistance comes when we recognize that we are working with more than physiology. We are emotional, intellectual, spiritual beings.

Now it is time for woman to recognize her own value. Our emotions, which we have been programmed to deny, are extremely powerful. When your imbalanced female organs call your attention, listen with your inner hearing. As far back as I remember I rushed through life. When you rush, your images of the past are viewed dismissively and become fuzzy. Life is far too sacred for such dismissal. If you take the time to be in the moment with whatever you are doing, every moment is precious. You know and experience the beauty and value of life, moment by moment and are thus able to look back and see magnificent memories you will cherish forever.

I was made to remember through my ordeal that when I operate by intuition, my intellect and emotional self move under guidance without running rampant in fear-based thinking. My meditation practice helps to connect me to that intuitive place. The practice of being in silence lead by the power of conscious breath helps me remain in the present where I know each moment is perfect and helps me accept those transformative times in my life. I knew that I was laboring to bring forth something magnificent that I had called into existence. I didn't know what it would look like, but I was certain the outcome was for my highest good. My intuition brought me through the journey and continues to direct my life. It taught me to know my empowerment and value as woman. Although, I am depended upon to nurture and heal humankind, I now understand that in order to do that I must *place the oxygen mask over my face first before assisting others*. There is, in fact, much to be remembered by looking back. What looked like the weakness of women through my childish eyes I now recognize as the quiet strength and guidance offered up by woman when she knows just how empowered she is. No roaring is necessary.

Resurrecting the Muse

Reach out to empowered women over the next 7 days. Think of women in your personal life that you feel are in touch with themselves as empowered women aligned with their innate nature as a woman. Women who you believe follow their intuitive guidance.

Contact at least 2 of them and let them know how they have touched your life.

If you don't know 2 such women personally send a communication to a public figure for whom you have the same feeling and awareness.

The communication will benefit you as you recognize empowerment demonstrated through woman. You will recognize the availability of such empowerment for yourself. If you can see it in someone else it must exist within you.

Use your journal to capture the emotions and insights that you experienced in this process.

In the very beginning of her life, the girl-child has direct access to the spirit of life...Her imagination is free for a time. She needs no priest or teacher to describe "God" to her. Spirit erupts spontaneously in colorful and unique expressions. God is Grandma, the twinkling evening star, the gentle breeze that washes across her face, the peaceful, quiet darkness after everyone has fallen asleep, and all the colors of the rainbow. Because she is a girl, her experience and expression of spirit is uniquely feminine. It flows from her essence as naturally as breath. The spirit of the universe pulsates through her. She is in love with herself.

Patricia L. Reilly,
"Imagine A Woman In Love With Herself"

CHAPTER THREE

Our Intuitive Power: The Spirit Of Life

"You're weird!" I heard those two words often as I was growing up. It wasn't until early adulthood that I understood the meaning. Apparently, I thought a little outside the box. I just never could see the box into which people wanted me to fit. I didn't like coloring inside the lines. I spent a lot of time inside my own head, not always wishing to interact with the outer world. People called that being shy. Other than the discomfort of having to accept that others felt something was *not right* about me, and that I was supposed to behave differently for the comfort of others, I really liked it inside.

When I was about eight, I created my own form of meditation. No one taught me about meditation. I never heard the word as a child. I didn't know anything of

Divine guidance or inner connection. However, intuitively I felt a connection to *something*. Whenever I was afraid, anxious or worried I went upstairs to my bedroom, turned off the lights, got into bed under the covers and placed the palms of my hands tightly over my eyes. My intention was to make it as pitch black as possible. I sat still until out of the deep darkness came *The Light*. The moment that I saw that Light, I knew there was nothing to fear. There was no need for worry; I was comforted.

My nickname in high school was Frantic Fran. I was addicted to sugar. My mother tells me she discovered that the babysitter put it in our food to get my sister, brother and me to eat dinner. I must admit I was pretty high strung. I used to eat *Chips Ahoy* cookies a bag at a time. My lifestyle was not a healthy one. Vegetables were just something that sat on my plate next to the meat. I never ate salads and sugar was making me crazy!

I let go of my "meditation" practice when I entered college. I thought my roommate might think I was a little...weird. That's when I began to find "enlightenment" through experimenting with substances. I had opened myself to inner guidance through my creative meditation practice and remained conscious of its availability. I was naturally a very internal being; inner guidance stopped me from going overboard in my 20's and 30's. I lived on the edge, but there was something that kept me from crossing the line away from wellbeing into total personal destruction. If I began to slip away that *voice* began screaming to be heard, *"Don't have that fourth drink! Have you noticed that smoking three packs of cigarettes per day is affecting your breathing? You can't smoke pot all day and actually believe you're productive! That cocaine might make you feel good tonight, but you'll pay two days later when you feel like crap. No, don't touch it; not heroin!"* When I tried to push that voice away something always pulled me back. Even through my "destructive" behavior I always knew I was safe and protected.

One evening a neighbor rang my doorbell. He had just arrived home from a Transcendental Meditation class. I had never seen him so excited. He shared his transformational experience with me and I thought he was a bit insane! I rushed him away that evening. Yet, much to my surprise, I awoke the next morning curious to know more. I came to recognize my friend's visit that evening as divine intervention, marking the beginning of my conscious journey inward. That same week I attended my first meditation class. I still remember how strange the facilitators appeared---"so zoned out" and a bit too peaceful for what I was used to. I remember thinking, "I want the benefit of what they're teaching, but I don't want to be like them." My first meditation was amazing! I felt clear. I was awakened, later realizing I had been walking through life asleep. From that moment I dedicated myself to the practice of meditation. No matter where I was, I stopped what I was doing for twenty minutes twice a day and meditated. Suddenly, my world was peaceful and calm. My meditation buddy and I gathered a group of friends and began practicing silent communication along with our practice of meditation. We would sit and concentrate on a number or color then write down what came to us. To our amazement, the majority of us would have the same information written down each time. It was our way of proving to ourselves that there was something significant about this place within: one mind, perhaps. With continued practice I began to believe that the gut feelings, which I had experienced, were what people referred to as inner knowing, there to guide my life. I committed to paying attention to it.

I became increasingly conscious of what was good for my body and what it rejected. My cravings for unhealthy food vanished. It took awhile, but eventually I was done with cigarettes, not because I was concerned about my health, but because I began to realize I no longer needed them. Smoking was a nervous habit and I had found something more effective. I became a very strict vegetarian and then settled into a more gentle balanced way of healthy eating. I found myself drawn to the "occult" section of bookstores, where I discovered yoga books. I fell in love with yoga the day of my first practice, even with my failed early attempts at sitting in lotus and standing on my head. I came to the realization that I hadn't really changed; I just became a more in sync version of me. As if some higher, calmer existence wanted me to be connected to it. No "zoning out", thank goodness!

We are programmed by our society and our families to view life from external circumstances, situations and conditions. This outside programming is a method for controlling behavior. It becomes a barrier to the inner guidance system. In my spiritual counseling practice it has become quite clear that each of us carries beliefs which operate from the behind-the-scene shadows. These beliefs lead our lives without engaging our conscious awareness. They are not within our thought process, but can run our lives unless we consciously live from the gut feelings, that inner guidance. Humankind tends to buy into beliefs without questioning whether they ring true for ourselves, especially when we are young. We believe that others know what is true. If we go to our guidance first, listen to the inner nudging, the still, small voice, it will act as a barrier to adverse conditions, situations and circumstances. It will provide us the security that gives us the peacefulness to know that although we might feel the fear, anxiety or discomfort from outside circumstances they don't control us. It is only our perception that allows those circumstances to overpower our lives and perhaps push us to make harmful choices. If we remember to remember the blueprint given at the point of our emergence, we breathe and are aware of an undeniable connection to the Creator of life that will shift our perception and give a new awareness to what is actually of importance for our greater unfoldment.

It is a difficult concept to grasp that there is an observer that lives through and connects every living thing. It is called by many names: God, Goddess, Spirit, Source, Divine Feminine, etc. It is that from whence everything comes, that which creates all. It is the very essence of all. It is what we are in alignment with when we feel joyful and peaceful. It is that from which we observe and it is that which is being observed. It is the Spirit of our lives.

The availability of this alignment is shown to us through the blueprint that we spoke of earlier. When giving birth, woman is tuned into the frequency of this Creative Intelligence. When woman synchronizes her breath with the flow of the progression of labor (not trying the impossible task of focusing on something outside) she surrenders to the nowness of an intuitive process and can witness the workings of the Creator, which is in full control. There is nothing in her thought process, ego, personality or might that can birth a child. She is a vessel for something that takes over her being as she surrenders to an intuitive, primordial process over which she has no control. She is not the doer, consciously thinking, but rather is witness to this magnificent occurrence, simultaneously grounded in the experience of the pain associated with giving birth. Often there is a primal scream that comes from a place, a voice, with which she is unfamiliar. She allows this painful take over for the higher purpose of co-creating new life. It is a privilege and an honor to be used in this way. She moves her egotistical self aside for the creative process to take form, allowing herself to be used as a conduit for Spirit. And then she forgets. She begins to believe she is in control of this emergent being. Under the influence of the collective unconsciousness of a society driven by the need to control, she forgets that it is impossible to control another. She forgets that she was never in control. She had no control over how the manifestation of life would take place. It was not under her influence when the manifestation would occur or even what its appearance would be. She definitely had no control over whether or not one of her hundreds of thousands of eggs would be selected as the one to magnetize that one in hundreds of millions of sperm cells from man to allow this magnificent co-creation of Life. She passes the collective unconsciousness onto the child and the circle continues. The coexistence of pain and joy is forgotten.

Life is birthed through synchronicity. It is my understanding of Truth that there really are no coincidental occurrences. When discomfort, pain or anxiety occurs it has a purpose providing me an opportunity to give birth to newness. Therefore, what seems a separate circumstance is actually a synchronistic occurrence necessary for my growth and expansion...my evolution. That is the way our universe operates and is the way the adventure we call life unfolds. That is the way in which we connect with the Spirit of Life. In the blueprint, pain appears indicating the new life has outgrown the comfort of the womb. Pain appears in our lives as an indication that we are living in a world too small. This painful communication is giving us the opportunity for the emergence of a higher activation of potential. Life offers many possible outcomes to any given situation. Sometimes we are unaware of what is available until we feel the pain and discomfort of a world too small, which urges us forward to embrace a greater way of living. Humankind exists because of the birthing process. All new ideas that we want to experience during our lives come into being through a sometimes painful birthing process. Yet, when we give it full sway, understanding that the attempt to control is limiting, we witness the Perfect Spirit of our Lives.

Woman is wired for this intuitive process. It is written in her DNA to allow intuition. Yet, we question whether or not we are intuitive. Books, speakers, gurus and counselors can inspire you to intuit your truth, but the only way to know it as your truth is through deep listening inside. You can read all the books, hear all the speakers, follow every guru, but the only way to know is to deeply listen within your own being. Your Truth is spoken to you, for you and through you. *The key to unlocking the doorway to your inner knowing is through the disciplined practice of inner listening...meditation.*

There are many meditation methods to take you there, but the most important goal of meditation is to have no goal. We spend hours in our intellect, ego and personality. Meditation quiets the self long enough to hand the reigns to the intuitive nature where we let go of our control and take time to allow. When we tune in, we hear a voice that speaks clearly. It can be heard only when we turn down the volume of our ego-centered way of living. It speaks ever so softly, but the attempt to tune it out or ignore its presence will form a choir of angels to raise the volume and get your attention. It is always vying for your attention because you were created for It to be seen and heard as you. It is counting on you, Woman, to be its voice, guiding the way. Woman is wired for intuitive knowing and her wisdom is an unmistakable necessity: assisting others into alignment with the Spirit of Life.

Resurrecting the Muse

Record your intuitive insights every day for the next 7 days, at least.

Pay attention to the ways in which you receive intuitive guidance. Is it visual, auditory, kinesthetic, a combination?

Test yourself:

- When the phone rings see if you know who it is before answering.

- Notice red flag feelings that come from deep inside.

- Sit, close your eyes and send your energy to someone that you know. Speak with them and find out if they don't say, "I was just thinking of you!"

Take note of the intuitive insights that you receive. Keep track of all of them in your journal for at least 7 days.

Most importantly, remember that you are intuitive and begin to use your intuitive power and rely on it.

Read a book or take a class on meditation. If you are already familiar with the practice make it a discipline. It is the passageway to a clearer connection with your intuitive guidance.

I am the Ocean...it is not the moon that calls me to shore...it is I who awaken the
moon and calls him down...and rest in his light...that I may dream
I am a cloud...I float above all else...I bring shade from the sun...I cool your coffee...I
make shapes to your stories
I am your future
When the waters embrace me...when the moon glows down...you clearly see me shin-
ing I...Am...A Jewel...I shine
I Am
Priceless...Incomparable...Undeniable...Wonderful
Me
Forever and Always Dreaming
Of you

—Nikki Giovanni
"I Am The Ocean"

CHAPTER FOUR

Our Economic Power: True Wealth

90% of the time the final decision for the purchase of a home-the single largest purchase most make in a lifetime-lies in the hands of the woman. Realtors are full of assurances that if the woman is happy with the home, there will be peace. Car manufacturers target women even when the car will be driven by the man. A very financially secure friend, decided to purchase a new Porsche for himself without his wife's knowledge. When he pridefully showed her his purchase she "strongly suggested" he return it in support of the bigger picture.

Men might not really understand why they are dependent on woman's decision making. Woman processes in a way that takes in many aspects of her being. She sets the tone in conjunction with her sixth sense through her innate organization and management skills. She is caregiver for the home, family members, friends, children, and her partner/spouse while managing her own job or career. In fact, because woman handles so many tasks simultaneously it is proven that she has developed a brain structure different from males who are not wired for this type of juggling act. Yet, woman doesn't stop to credit herself for her many talents. Although society depends on her, seeking her guidance and direction, woman is not acknowledged for being a powerful force. In fact, she is made to believe quite the opposite.

Woman has moved away from remembering that she co-creates life with the Divine. She has forgotten that the children look to her for nurturing, to speak to them of their strength, their power, their goodness. She has dismissed the fact that man needs her compassion, her ability to connect, her heartfelt communication; even when he isn't aware that it is what he is seeking. Woman has never stopped being the lifeline for others. She has forgotten that innately she is the Muse. It is her nature, demonstrated in the birthing process through which each human incarnates. The need for connection to woman never vanishes. While not consciously aware of her essential value, she experiences depletion within, which causes an inability to provide enough nourishment for all to thrive. Woman has come to the place where she behaves as if in agreement with a collective unconsciousness which defines her as less than and not enough. She has come to forget that she must feed herself in order to have enough to feed others. The truth is that woman's value is undeniable. Her participation in the shaping and creation of our society is a major contribution to its strength, especially its economic strength. In fact, in the US women make up half the workforce and the number of women in the workforce is growing all around the world.

There is a lie told, through the fact that women don't earn equal pay to men, that women are indeed less capable than men. Woman does tricks for the carrots dangled before her, in an attempt to be accepted. Our society's actions come from impoverished thinking, the belief that there is not enough for everyone to share in the abundance. That thinking and belief creates woman's impoverished life. It is *only* our thinking and our belief system, certainly not the truth of woman. Deep within her core she remembers. Her truth lives within the stillness which she so seldom feels while her attention is seduced by the outer world. I don't suppose any woman truly believes that she is innately less capable than her male counterpart.

An inherent stress comes along with being an adult in a female body. We are expected by society, our families, partners, our jobs, and ourselves to give to the point of overwhelming exhaustion. Women find it very difficult to put themselves into their lives. When working in the corporate world, I recall asking my children to give me 20 minutes to myself when I returned home from work before beginning my second job as mother and wife. That time alone in the inner sanctuary allowed me to reemerge peaceful and calm to "mother" my children. It assisted me to let go of the influence of the collective belief about whom and what I am as a woman. I was able to come home to *me* and feel my Truth. In a twenty-four hour day most women, especially women with families, think of themselves for no more than a fleeting moment, if at all. When we do consider ourselves, it is generally in reference to what someone desires from us. How do we conduct ourselves the way indoctrination dictates that we should? How can we dress and make ourselves look the way we are programmed to look and dress? How do we fit these round bodies into those square, octagonal and triangular holes? The expressed value of woman is linked with what she is in relationship to others; having no concern for what she requires for herself. Women put their needs, wants and creativity on hold to assist their partners in their creative endeavors or their bosses with goals for the company or their children through all undertakings of life. I have women friends in 30-year marriages whose children are now adults. These mothers are paralyzed, unable to make the tiniest step towards their own self-expression. They cry out to find their dreams, but are no longer able to hear the longing of their hearts. Women's bodies reflect that we are living outside our true nature. Is this the reason that heart disease is the number one killer of women in our country? Woman's heart is her strength and she is programmed to dismiss it. Women are plagued with fibroids, endometriosis, ovarian cysts and on and on. Younger and younger women are being diagnosed with reproductive disorders. What does this say about the way we women are living our lives and ignoring our essential selves? The removal of one uterus, two fallopian tubes, two ovaries and 26 lymph nodes along with receiving 2 units of blood and five weeks of daily radiation therapy throughout my entire torso region are the ultimate evidence of my former impoverishment.

The lack of value placed on the *essential* nature of woman has impoverished our culture in innumerable ways. Our world thirsts for power without remembering that empowerment comes from within. The discrediting of the intuitive voice of woman causes a communication shut down within her which is reflected into our society. Reliance on the intellect clouds the inner guidance. The dismissal of woman's emotions dishonors her heart. The Creator knew what it was doing when it designed woman just as she is. It is because of the way she processes that she is relied on to make 80% of all decisions for her family, proof that economic power rests in the hands of women in our society. When woman attempts to suppress her essential nature, it stops her flow and her body becomes toxic. This toxic state is reflected back to us through the impurity of the water, the food, soil and air of our contaminated world. We've come to associate power with the attainment of wealth. The thought of wealth conjures up images of mansions, cars, travel, money, money, money; the things for which we feverishly strive. Power in our society is equated to economic power or "power over"-- a method of control causing woman to forget.

All that has taken place in our history has brought us to this point where we are co-creating a new story as we move forward. History teaches that once upon a time, society was female-centered and women were honored for their co-creation of life, raising children, creating art and technology and making intuitive-based decisions for the community in which they lived and led. Then the time came during which we moved into the male-centered society with which we are quite familiar. We now have the opportunity to create a history that honors all. For this movement to be completed, women must find their woman-ness, their balance. When woman moved into the workforce it felt necessary for her to take on the attitude, the character, the mannerism of maleness. It was the way to be accepted and remain in that world. She has learned well. Women run corporations, hold high government positions, and have wealth and stature in our society. Soon she will be POTUS. Woman can continue to enjoy her accomplishments while standing in her empowerment and demonstrating *True Wealth*.

Her inner-knowing will tell her each step to take moving through life, careers, and relationships. Woman is highly intuitive. Her inner guidance is felt in her body as gut feeling and through her emotions as knowing information without the process of reasoning. It is referred to as Woman's Intuition and Mother Wit. She might ask herself how often she is consciously in this place of knowing because when she allows herself to flow with her intuitive knowing she is able to create magic, making a way out of no way. When woman is in her empowered self she attracts her desire by standing unwaveringly in the awareness and acceptance of her value. Woman's mind and emotions are extremely powerful. When in alignment with them, she will enjoy the feeling of empowerment.

When she reveals the Truth, which has been covered by lies, she know that she is a powerful alchemist who can focus her intentions and attract her heart's desires for her benefit and the benefit of all. When woman stops abandoning herself for the indulgence of her loved ones, she remembers her importance and acknowledges it by pursuing her heartfelt dreams and reclaiming her worth. We are being called to walk in a balanced state which cannot exist without this remembrance and reclaiming of balance within. The woman who knows that she lives in a world of endless possibility demonstrates *True Wealth*, not concerned with the fluctuations on Wall Street. Since society looks to woman for guidance, imagine the balance created as she embodies empowerment and the True wealth that comes from remembering that she lives in a limitless universe that does not need her impoverished feelings and beliefs. We will manifest balance in our society when the guidance so sought after from woman comes from her alignment with balance without the desire to control behavior. Women are the nurturers to our society, the co-creators of life, the Dreamweaver, the inspirational and motivational force. Woman is the Muse for everyone. It is the essential nature of woman. There is no greater wealth than hearing one's own truth, trusting and revealing it.

Resurrecting the Muse

Take time each day to be aware of the value that you contribute to society.

Spend time each day reviewing in your mind the decisions which you are regularly depended upon to make. Do you make decisions for a shared household, for children, on your job? How do your decisions affect the economy of our society? Acknowledge your significance.

Embody the feeling of economic value by giving back to yourself financially.

Go to the library, bookstore or online to find books that will assist you in building your personal financial wealth if that is an area of concern for you. If it is not, assist another woman in learning to build her financial wealth.

Write your discoveries in your journal.

Show me how you take care of business without letting business determine who you are.
When the children are fed but still the voices within and around us shout that soul's desires have too high a price, let us remind each other that it is never about the money.
And when the sound of all the declarations of our sincerest intentions has died away on the wind, dance with me in the infinite pause before the next great inhale
of the breath that is breathing us all into being, not filling the emptiness from the outside or from within.
Don't say, "Yes!"
Just take my hand and
dance with me.

—Oriah Mountain Dreamer
"The Dance"

CHAPTER FIVE

Our Inspirational Power: The Breath Of Life.

"I just don't have time" is the lie we tell ourselves. If it was a matter of one more thing our loved ones needed, we could make that time magically appear. Yet, our own needs are pushed aside. I continuously hear from women, "I'm tired! I have to handle everything or else it won't get done." We deal with the stress of being women in a male-oriented world. Working mothers fight through traffic to get our children to school and ourselves to work, after making breakfast for family, only to rush through traffic to return home, prepare dinner, help with homework, pay bills, etc. You know the drill! The saying, "A woman's work is never done" has never been truer or more detrimental than it is today. We are out of breath!!

Woman has become so preoccupied with the *doing* of her life that she cannot hear the desires from her heart. When and if she does hear those whispers she isn't tuned in enough to see the steps shown and follow the guidance because to truly listen requires being in the present moment. Her mind is preoccupied with accomplishing tasks. She is far too dependent on the intellect to feel the guidance which determines moment by moment which steps to take along the path to her most beneficial, highest good. Conscious breath is the prescribed medicine.

I thought I was taking all the correct steps in self-care, but no one told me to breathe! Every week I had a two-hour massage. However, my massage therapist could confirm that I flew into that room, threw off my clothes and jumped onto the table. I let go while I was there, but the moment that massage was over I leaped back into the pressures of my day never taking time to truly pause. I rushed through life. I was in a hurry every place I went. "I must get to work extra early to get everything done. I have to get to that appointment on time." I arranged my work schedule to leave each day to pick up my daughters from school, take them home to the nanny, and return to my job. I knew that at the end of the school day was the time they wanted to spend talking; precious moments that would be lost by the time I came home from work. While I don't regret the time I dedicated to my family, in retrospect, I could have added *me* to my list of priorities. I tried, but I didn't know how.

I practiced yoga and meditation daily before my family was awake, but once they arose my life went into full swing. I made breakfast and lunch for my children (which at some point they informed me they didn't need me to do). It was my unconscious way of letting go of the guilt I felt for being such a busy mother. I drove them to school and picked them up, attended every performance, took them to social events with their friends, who in turn were always welcomed in our home and at our dinner table. On several occasions during their teen years I opened my home to their friends who were unable to communicate with and live in the same space with their parents. I was available for all my children- to talk with them and for them to talk with me, nevertheless, harboring guilt because I knew deep inside I was not fully there. I had a million things going through my mind at all times. I did not know how to truly stop and breathe; to pause and allow myself to experience the nowness of the moment. I didn't know how to truly live in gratitude for the present moment and all of its wonderment and magnificence. You know, stopping to *smell the roses*. I was a pro at going through the motions not realizing that I wasn't taking anything in.

Woman gives of her sustenance without replenishing nourishment for her own wellbeing. *If the pregnant mother does not provide enough for self, as well as the dependent baby, the baby will not thrive and the mother's well-being will suffer.* When Woman undervalues who she is, she allows herself to be undervalued by society. When she demonstrates the inability to care for her needs and protect her heart, she shows her children, family, co-workers and friends that she is unimportant. When she allows her spouse or partner's needs to stand in front of her own she demonstrates that she is not worth valuing. When she establishes no boundaries at work stress places her health in harm's way and when she gives her sexuality with no understanding of its importance-her sexuality heals- there is an emptiness experienced through sexual expression. Living in this scripted way causes the world to reflect her lack of harmony. The universe is not judging and discerning. It is vibrating where we vibrate and woman's energy is extremely powerful. If we believe what is demonstrated in the beginning, feminine energy egg attracts masculine energy sperm. The sperm finds its way to her because her chemistry changes to guide him. Feminine energy attracts and newness is always being birthed through that attraction. At the level which we vibrate (through our thoughts and our feel-ings) creation occurs and that vibration manifests in the outer world. We live in a society which has lost connection with respect, compassion and conviction. Our planet is at war, ravaged by quakes, volcanoes, hurricanes and tsunamis; evidence of tension, hostility, violence and dis-ease within the expression of humankind. It is not my desire to blame women for all the woes of the world. There is no right or wrong, no blame or fault. However, my intuitive voice tells me when Woman real-izes and honors her powerful role; society will reflect more harmony and balance.

When Woman includes herself in nurturing and care giving, she evidences self-love and respect. It is from this perspective that she is able to effectively inspire all of those who depend on her for their own care and guidance. Woman is a ben-eficial presence, promoting healing when she is aligned with that place from which she is fed. When she feeds upon the expansive nature of breath her etheric heart expands and she moves forward aligned with her inner spiritual power. She is then able to cradle humankind in her lap and stroke the brow of all who are turning to her for comfort. She inspires clarity through answers given from alignment with her intuitive knowing. She enhances a world, which looks to woman to reflect the beauty and harmony of the universe.

We literally *must* learn to schedule ourselves into our day. If we place our-selves on our schedules, we will find that there *is* time enough. Time for self can appear in many ways, from going outside the home to an exercise class, taking a walk or having a massage; to in-home activities, such as meditation, time on the yoga mat or a long soak in the tub; all done consciously with gratitude for the mo-ment. Most importantly, we realign with our inspirational power when we are in community with other women. We give to the men and the children. Women must give to each other unconditional love, hope and strength. Whatever the choices, it is imperative that we include ourselves as a part of what we consider to be impor-tant in our lives. We must take pause. The time commitment does not need to be large. To hear our hearts we must breathe consciously. Breath brings the calm, the stillness, the remembrance of our magnificent empowerment. Every living thing in creation breathes. Breath is the indication that life exists. The very first breath in human life takes place inside the womb. Life in its very essence takes place inside the womb. Woman co-creates Life. When we remember to breathe we return to our sense of being whole and allow the perfect flow of life. When we breathe we are in the moment, not living in future moments. When we consciously breathe we can feel that which inspires us and can dip into that wellspring on behalf of others. Woman, you are of such significance that humankind cannot continue without you as its co-creator. You have the power to inspire lives. You deserve time to breathe!

Resurrecting the Muse

Practice this synchronized breathing every day for the next 7 days, at least. (It will take 10-20 minutes)

Sit with your back straight and your eyes closed. You may sit on the floor or in a chair. It is important to be comfortable. Begin by focusing on your breath and following its natural rhythm without attempting to control the breath.

As you exhale, think, "fifty".
As you inhale think, "forty-nine",
Exhale, "forty-eight"
Inhale, "forty-seven"
Exhale, "forty-six"...and so on..

Count backward on both the inhale and the exhale until you reach "twenty".
Then count only the exhales.

Silently count "twenty" as you exhale.
Then instead of counting "nineteen" on the inhale, just inhale.
With the next exhalation count "nineteen"...and so on
Until you reach zero.

When you reach zero stop counting, while staying in-tune with the rhythm of your breath without attempting to control it.
Stay with this rhythm for a few moments and realize how relaxed and in alignment you feel.

(If you lose track of whether or not to inhale or exhale on the even/odd number, don't concern yourself. Pick up wherever you are. If you lose track of your number just pick a number that you believe might be it. Losing track means you are experiencing the benefits of the practice.)

Write your discoveries in your journal.

The world has nothing for me
Nothing much you understand
So for sure it's up to me to bring water to a dry land
No more sitting in a dark room
Searching for a reason
That God would bring me to this Earth
For such a violent season
But to bear the song of love
Or to bear the gift of prophecy
It's time to sing the truth that I understand
And bring water to this dry land

Rickie Byars Beckwith
"Water to a Dry Land"

CHAPTER SIX

Our Uplifting Power: Wisdom

When women moved into the male workforce the dynamics of our lives shifted drastically and a necessary retraining occurred. Entrapped in fear, sense of self was taken away. Women wielded so much power within the home and community but it was not welcomed in man's workforce. While men still, conceded most decisions in matters of the home to her they seemed unable to allow her to exercise such power in the workplace or public sphere.

Woman walked into the lion's den when she left home to play with the boys. She was made to feel inadequate because she was forced to learn a new way of operating in the autonomous world run by men with their own sense of power. Woman was forced to adapt and a necessary struggle ensued for her to be considered equal in this unfamiliar territory. Forgetting her innate wisdom and tendency to motivate and inspire, Woman bought into a belief system which told her that if she didn't play by the rules she had to take her little red wagon and go home. We forgot what every Spiritual Being knows...the discomfort doesn't make us fail, but in the end helps us embody what we've called forth and provides us an opportunity to heal old wounds and give birth to newness.

Over generations woman has embodied at the cellular level that she is not good enough and must adapt in order to please and be accepted by man. Though counterintuitive to woman's natural state of empowerment it exists, nonetheless, in the female collective unconsciousness. If we don't consciously align with our own Truth, we find ourselves believing what others-often men-tell us is true. The work world requests our intelligence not our compassion. Upon entry into it, we began to function in environments where solutions come through analytical process and not from innate wisdom, compassion and healing. Goals, quotas and complimentary reviews are achieved when we fit the mold leaving no room for creativity and inward reflection that typify our essential nature; the place from which our female wisdom springs. It becomes our natural state to live in the future according to our schedules with detachment from the present moment. Yet, it is in present moment where our wisdom and sense of wholeness are most apparent.

Women entering the scene of the "Boys Club" changed the face of man's work world completely. Her presence eventually rewrote the labor laws to accommodate her needs, causing man's resentment toward woman. There is an unspoken question of how one should function in the man's world while remaining feminine, without calling inappropriate attention to femininity or using its power for personal gain. The workplace can leave us uncertain whether or not to behave like men or women. Woman must master the skill of demonstrating assertiveness without being considered a *bitch*. There are unwritten rules in the Boys Club that forever deeply affect woman. The rules change from one place of employment to the next; from one social event to another; sometimes moment by moment. There are no warning signs. I learned through my career in advertising how to play hard with the boys. When I achieved my greatest level of career success the feminine energy was in play, but the masculine was at the forefront big time. I endured a tremendous amount of stress from the imbalance. The state of overwhelm and over commitment experienced by most women causes our adrenal glands to produce too much of the hormones cortisol and estrogen. Estrogen dominance is the major cause of most female disorders including breast, uterine and ovarian cancer.

Often because she has so mastered the art of adaptation, woman doesn't even realize herself that she is shape shifting, hiding and shrinking. I observed women in my corporate workplace repress their feelings to adapt to the environment, silencing their voices for supposed acceptance. Sadly, women frequently turn their backs on each other when they perceive another woman as a threat to her success, not just in the work environment, but in relationships of all kinds. Though, countless times I was present when women in my office rallied around one of our sisters in the ladies room as she allowed her woman-ness to reveal itself through tears. We, in turn resurrected our Muse, if only for a moment, as we inspired her back into alignment with her joy. Deep in the female psyche often lies the belief that woman is in competition with others of her gender. Women need each other to assist in the remembering that competitiveness is masculine energy which has it's place in our female lives, yet, at the core of our being is the Divine Feminine energy desiring to be at the forefront guiding through our intuitive wisdom and unconditional love because we are all One Life, One Love.

Our tenuous beginnings in the labor force have fostered a belief which has become entrenched in the female collective unconscious that woman should hide her power and appear less capable. The struggle to adapt results in woman's conflicted feelings and begging for acceptance. At times she fought for recognition from those who held the golden keys while dismissing both parts of her and other women. Yet in her essential nature woman wants everyone to feel good, even at her own detriment. Coexisting in the collective consciousness is bitterness in man toward woman because she invaded his domain. These feelings arose in humankind because of the circumstances at a particular point in our history. These false beliefs run rampant in our society as if they are the truth. Yet, they are not truth.

As employees, spouses, parents, daughters we give our all until there is nothing left for us, an imbalance and confusion we ourselves create-- because we love; it is our way of nurturing and care taking inextricable from our essential nature. It is our nature to uplift and help others to feel their value. There is, indeed a feminine nature just as there is a masculine nature. Science tells us that males typically use the left side of the brain for thought processing and communicate from solution oriented thinking while females tend to use both right and left brained thinking in communication. The right brain connects with the body more than the left side of the brain. Thus, woman is thinking and feeling communication at the same time. When honoring her essential nature she is responsive to her emotions, understanding that she can tap into guidance beyond her intellect, resulting in her decision-making being more powerful and accurate because it comes from connection with her mind, body and emotions in synchronicity. In a male driven society this processing is depended upon. It is the reason woman is still targeted in advertising campaigns as the decision maker. Yet, woman is not encouraged to understand her value. Society looks to woman to tell it how to spend its money, organize and schedule its time and raise its children while she doubts her own inner wisdom.

Woman has become confused while wearing the masculine cloak. This confusion is evidenced in a world starving for compassion and kindness. Woman is disconnected from her heart space while she orchestrates the lives of those around her. We are witnessing a society where children don't know the benefit of unconditional love because we've lost sight of self-love. We pass this dis-ease down through the generations. If she doesn't fit the image expected of her by masculine society, woman takes on woundedness and her self-talk becomes about not being okay. Sometimes the confusion goes unnoticed because woman's attention is called to everyone and everything outside of her. Women turn their backs on other women—a natural by-product women experience while trying to survive in a competition-based world. We cannot afford to show disrespect to each other. Society does that enough without our help. All women experience some sense of depletion, despite the fact that we are all powerful, creative, wise beings. When we are able to see that truth in ourselves, we should be able to recognize it in other women and the end result is that we are all uplifted. This upliftment assists us in standing strong in our Truth individually and collectively. Only from this connection with our innate nature can we make the decisions on which our society depends-and from a place of wisdom instead of fear and conditioning.

We must heal our wounds and thus assist in healing the wounds of our society. Women are being asked to acknowledge and align with their true essence, not only for the benefit of those who walk on earth as women, but for all human life. There is a clear calling which requires women to recognize our value as the embodiment of the Sacred. We can facilitate that by coming together in community as women, which is the most natural way for women to co-exist, as seen in other societies around the world. We come together to communicate and uplift. The energy being called forth is one which represents wholeness, not competition, separation or compartmentalization. When we allow guidance from an inner knowing, we reveal the Divine, Sacred, Feminine aspect which is inclusive of all parts of the whole and medicine for us all. The Divine Feminine is asking us to see her feminine energy as compassion, empowerment, love, creativity, abundance, respect...all the goodness of life.

By calling the earth "mother" we innately recognize the earth as feminine energy. She is the womb through which all plant life comes and where nourishment occurs. It is the female's womb through which human life is birthed. Woman is to human life what Mother Earth is to all life. The earth is sacred. Woman's womb is sacred. We have ravaged the earth, abused it, brutalized it, but we cannot destroy it. It will quake to recalibrate itself. It will explode to find rebalance and move again into a state of synchronicity, as will woman. When she becomes toxic from disrespect and mistreatment her attention is called back, sometimes through pain, to remember that the feminine is sacred energy.

It is not necessary for woman to seek validation from anyone outside of herself. We do not need approval nor do we need to discredit the system that has had its purposeful existence. We do not need to male bash or believe in the necessity of men understanding who we are as women. But above all, we must understand who we are. When we honor our sacredness, nature, true essence, others will understand who we are. We offer a medicine, which heals the planet when we recognize and live life in harmony with that essence. There is a necessary recalibration being called forth for woman to stand in her essential nature, just as Mother Earth will shake us up to stay true to hers.

Resurrecting the Muse

Plan time just for you to be uplifted each day during the next 7 days.

Plan time for you.

You can have a massage, go for a walk, soak in a tub, get a pedicure, the choices are infinite.

The importance is that you find some activity that leaves you feeling uplifted and fortified.

On one of the days get together with other uplifting women to support them in embracing for themselves the value with which you've reunited.

Men themselves have wondered
What they see in me.
They try so much
But they can't touch
My inner mystery. When I try to show them,
They say they still can't see.
It's in the arch of my back,
The sun of my smile,
The ride of my breasts,
The grace of my style.
I'm a woman
Phenomenally.
Phenomenal woman,
That's me.

Maya Angelou,
"Phenomenal Woman"

CHAPTER SEVEN

Our Sexual Power:
Oneness

All of humankind has its first home in the womb. Woman represents home. That is the mystery of woman, the strength of her attraction, the power of her sexuality. Man seeks connection with the sacredness of woman, largely not even realizing that he is healed by the medicine carried within her energetic being. Within the body of woman, Spirit incarnates through an intuitive process in which humankind is richly nurtured and protected. Woman represents a comfort, which heals like the soothing of a lullaby. Energetically, man seeks this soothing embrace through sexual connection. Unfortunately, he frequently encounters the woman disconnected from her essential nature. When disconnected from her sense of empowerment; programmed by society, family and things outside of self; woman is not fully conscious of her magnetism and functions as a modern, formularized female. She enters sexual encounters looking for acceptance, validation and love. In a world which uses the media to create images in our minds of the perfect size to be, career to have, clothes to wear and car to drive, woman has been seduced by outside pressures attempting to manipulate her for financial gain; causing her to forget that within her DNA is the power to heal, regardless of her physical appearance or her discount store shoes. It is a known fact that man will lie, cheat and steal for the opportunity to connect sexually with woman. Her feminine energy is irresistible. It is natural for man to desire woman sexually; it is his innate nature. Yet, woman is taught to be offended by it rather than understand it is a way in which he worships and adores her. Though she is innately aware that sex in its essential nature is sacred and cannot be authentically experienced in external focus, she might agree to have sex in situations that are inappropriate, unfulfilling, or will in some way make her pay later emotionally -sex of regret. Because society has reduced woman to sex objects, rather than honoring her sacredness, she might encounter sexual situations from a place of unworthiness not realizing that during sexual connection man wants more than anything to adore her, to please her, to show her that he is worthy of her praise.

It is human nature for everyone to come to woman for her unconditional love, compassion and nurturing because it's where they began, inside of woman, being loved and nurtured unconditionally. When woman does not understand who she is innately, when she has been seduced, functioning under the control of the outer world, she loses sight of her value. She provides a place of love when she keeps her heart open to love. It is what is being sought even through sexuality. Man physically and energetically enters into that holy, sacred place of woman. When woman's heart is open and she is in kindness and compassion, she nurtures man and can help him to find the kindness and compassion within himself. I'm not speaking of situations where there is force as in rape. I'm speaking of the sexual encounters between man and woman when woman says, "Yes". Who she accepts into her space is dependent on how she feels about herself. Her approach to sexuality exemplifies who she believes herself to be and how much value she understands herself to have. A woman who knows her power allows into her space partners able to align with her in that divine nature. Her partner has the willingness and the potential and she allows entrance. Woman who does not know her innate nature and her empowerment and does not understand that she is here to heal through her love and her compassion because it is the love and the compassion that is being sought, even through sexuality, does not realize that she allows into her space those who do not honor the Truth of who and what she is. Being led by outside influence she believes that she doesn't have value other than what is physically between her legs. It is not the Truth. It is what is within the heart space that guides what comes through sexuality. Woman in touch with her essential nature is aware of her sexual magnetism because she understands its origin and her intrinsic value. When she is open to love and loving; not simply love for that partner, but living from an unconditional, compassionate agape love-the highest and purest form of love; she includes herself in the loving. Love is what she gives and that is how she heals.

The essential woman understands that there is a vibrational energy exchanged during sex and allows exchange of this energy only when it feels appropriate. She carries that sexual partner within her energetic self; his dis-ease or his love dependent upon where he exists. It is part of the confusion of sexuality when woman is not aware that because man enters into her body his energy moves inside of her and is released there. There is a connection energetically that carries on even when man has physically left the building. Woman walks around with his energy within her very being. They will feel each other. If she is feeling him from a place of love he will feel the love. However, even when she loves him dearly and feels he dearly deserves her love, it is important that woman consciously release that energy so that she can remember her own space, feeling her emotion separate from the energetic connection with that man. It is part of the reason that they say that men are "crazy makers". It is because we are walking around with them in our energy field. They must be released to themselves so that we can be released to ourselves continuing in the love.

People say they want intimacy in relationship without the vital, deeper understanding of what they actually seek. Intimacy occurs when one is energetically connected to another. One must first be connected to their own inner feelings. The emotional feeling self must accompany the physical and mental aspects of oneself in order to know intimacy. Although, it cannot be found in sex it can be experienced through it and sex can be an excellent expression of intimacy. Nothing on earth is a better example of the true sacredness of connection, intimacy and oneness than sex. It is no accident that through this connection human life is co-created. How could it be less than sacred?

Our approach to sex and the manner in which we experience and share sex evidence our beliefs about ourselves. When man is confused and feeling disassociated from his innate power and connects with the formularized female, sex is no more than a perfunctory act, a performance. However, when the participants remain inside of the intuitive feeling self, sexuality is potentially an authentic communion and an experience of bliss that is beyond simple pleasure. This bliss-filled experience occurs with the detachment from the intellect during what is felt as a sense of suspension, similar to the experience of meditation. In the height of sexual excitement, the individuals are fully in the now moment, connected to the breath, allowing themselves to be guided to oneness with ecstasy; oneness with something Divine which lives inside of each, revealing the sacred nature of sex. When our sexuality is expressed with this degree of awareness and alignment with Source it is recognized as sacred sexuality.•• When we are conduits for energy, as occurs during sacred sex, we promote healing within the energetic being of those both to and from whom that energy flows. There is a rebalancing that occurs. We are in a space of alignment with the highest part of ourselves, feeling a sense of oneness with the creator of life. Letting go of thinking, being fully present in the moment and allowing feeling to take place makes space for this experience; this sense of oneness. To experience ecstasy during sex, it is imperative to let the thinking mind rest and the sensations to be at the forefront and become fully at one with the moment. A woman must let go to experience orgasm, and in the same way, a man must let go to maintain an erection. In order for the vibratory feeling of Oneness to take over one must let go, experiencing the nowness of the present moment. Sex is an avenue for alignment with the Divine nature. The vibrational upliftment of energy experienced during sacred sex and the upliftment of energy experienced in conscious alignment with the Divine are one and the same.

The highest part of ourselves is always calling us home to conscious alignment with It. Sexual intimacy is a gateway to that at-one-ment. However, the energy is often confused. Everyone seeks to receive and express love. We search for it outside of ourselves forgetting that what we seek lies within. Because we live in a society which desires to control our actions we forget that we are guided from within. When we live from the inside out rather than allowing control from the outside in, we experience oneness with Life. The pathway to that oneness is through the recognition and acknowledgment of the Nowness of Life. We spend so much time connected with the dead past and the imagined future that we are unable to be fully present in the here and now. When we are living in memory of past moments of worry and fear those fears from the past become our present reality. When we are living in the anticipated moments of the future, we can be in anxiety and fear of being unable to achieve our desired reality. Fear becomes the driving force and what we fear is attracted into our lives. When we are present with what is occurring in the Now we are experiencing reality. In present moment there is never anything to fear. There is only the realization that each moment is absolutely perfect and everything that we need is available in the Now. No wonder humankind is so drawn to sexual expression. We long for the connection with the peace, stillness and joy experienced there in the loins of woman. It is a place of no past, no future.

When woman remembers her intrinsic value, man will understand that he is in the presence of Divine Feminine. He will allow alignment to take place within his being, just as it did when he was birthed. He will recognize through his feeling self that he is divine by nature. Therein lies the reawakening of conscious oneness, fostered by the resurrection of the muse who is living in her heart space. Sex is understood as sacred because humankind cannot think up, figure out or manufacture the ecstatic state known through this intimate experience. Sacred sex provides the feeling of intimacy. The feeling of intimacy provides the recognition of one energetic existence.

Resurrecting the Muse

Spend time communing with nature. Become fully aware of it. (10 – 15 minutes per day, at least)

Take in the beauty of a particular flower that calls to you.

Rather than noticing it and passing it by, be in the present moment with it. Just for a few moments.

Feel its perfection. Feel that you are just as perfect, trusting and giving as the flower.

Accept it as your truth, if only for these few moments.

Do this for a few moments each day for 7 days.

Be in the present moment with some form of nature; it could be a tree, your pet, an insect, it doesn't matter. Let the thought come to you what to choose and go with it.

On the 7th day, look into the mirror and take in your own perfection. Look into (not at) your eyes. Become aware that you are just as perfect at your core as the expressions of nature, which you have witnessed over the past 6 days.

There is a vitality, a life force, a quickening, that is translated through you into action. And because there is only one of you in all time, this expression is unique. And if you block it, it will never exist through any other medium and it will be lost. The world will not have it. It is not your business to determine how good it is, nor how valuable, nor how it compares to other expressions. It is your business to keep it yours, clearly and directly, to keep the channel open.

Martha Graham,
"Notebooks of Martha Graham"

CHAPTER EIGHT

Our Co-Creation Power: The Newness Of Life

What is it with human beings? We get a "gut" feeling, an intuitive hit-- and we ignore it. The feeling comes on more strongly, the inner voice speaks louder, making the message clearer and still, we ignore it. Life comes along and slaps us with a hard blow and we say, "How did this happen to me?"

Those hard blows which we encounter in our lives are not intended to cause suffering nor for us to run away from. We are not here on planet earth without a road map. Our gut feelings are meant to direct our path. Those intuitive hits are our guidance system encouraging our growth. When we follow, It assists us in creating new situations in our lives. Allowing creativity to flow is the manner through which we move away from stuck patterns so that growth occurs. Inner guidance is always nudging us toward our innate sense of creativity because it is the pathway to newness. We are meant to continue to grow, otherwise, we become stagnant. We're shown glimpses of the possibilities available to us. Yet, when we hear the urging from our inner voice moving us toward that vision, we frequently tune it out because we look at the vision shown and become overwhelmed by it. We believe we don't have the wherewithal to accomplish the task ahead when, in fact, we are being shown a picture of what is actually available to us if we simply take a step. We are always shown that first step. Taking one step will reveal the next. Step-by-step birthing something new is easy when we align with the creative energy within. There is a tendency to believe that we are the ones doing the creating, however, when an artist paints a picture, the author writes, the songstress sings; there is often a sense of "losing oneself" to the activity. There is a releasing and letting go; allowing something to come forth that dwells within. Creation occurs when we permit the highest part of us to operate *through* us. In those moments we are not in thought, worry, fear, anxiety, concern or attempting to figure anything out. We are letting our natural "juices" flow when we are in alignment with creativity, allowing visions to come forward. We tap into the inner space, just as the mother aligns inward with the flow of breath, not outward in thought, to allow the birth of a newborn child. The beauty of our inner guidance system is that it will continue to nudge, vying for our attention, until we listen and follow. If we do not take the steps indicated, following this guidance, we begin to feel as if we are suffering in our lives. We are not here to suffer, but pain is an inescapable part of the human experience. Just as a pain in the body is a tap on the shoulder to alert us to needed changes of habit, intuitive hits are awakening us to do something differently, to create new situations in our lives. The evolution of our planet depends on our ability to tap into the flow of creative energy to perceive the world in new ways. We must practice it in our personal lives. We will then look around and see how our world has changed because of it. Creation springs from right-brained, feminine energy, which is the essence of the nature of woman.

Connection with our sense of creativity breeds the newness of life. Newness comes through woman's magic, her ability to embrace pure potentiality via the dreams that are dreamt through her and brought into manifestation. Although she sometimes ignores it, woman knows that she has this gift. All of humankind knows her possession of this ability to conjure and evoke that Presence which creates perfect toes and fingers, hearing and sight inside woman's womb. She does not need to know the how of it, only her connection to it. Woman is a muse providing inspiration to all. It is the reason society looks to her for answers even when it denies that it does so. Deep inside, woman knows her Truth. The ability to bring forth newness, creative energy, has been imparted in her loins.

Woman's power to co-create is necessary for the ongoingness of life. Yet, we live within the lines drawn for us, fearful of stepping outside of them. Woman has become an active participant in our male-oriented society, which has resulted in her forgetting her connection with inner guidance. She has forgotten that her body moves in rhythm with the phases of the moon and dreams are placed inside of her; as co-creator with The Creator, to manifests newness. In a world operating in balance, woman shares her dreams with man who then directs them through his linear nature. Feminine energy and masculine energy work in conjunction to consciously create new life. However, if woman does not remember to remember who and what she is essentially we continue to recreate sameness. Life Itself can no longer tolerate the rape and pillage of woman's true nature. We must continue to evolve. The Divine Feminine is calling Woman's attention back to acknowledge feminine energy as sacred. She is asking woman to recognize the significance of her role as co-creator of life; acknowledging within herself why man is so frequently told, "Listen to the woman!" Whether she chooses to give birth through her womb or not, woman gives birth through her nature. Each month, in tempo with the moon she releases the potential for new life. Woman is empowered to co-create with Spirit life's most significant creation. She is the form through which newness comes. Woman, as the Muse, you assist those who live in intellectual pro-cess to embrace that which exists within and brings forth new ideas, new concepts, and new ways of existence when you reach into your knowingness and inspire others to reach into theirs. You are meant to dream the dreams that are brought into manifestation with masculine energy as your helpmate.

The Creator designed woman with a complex processing system which involves not only both hemispheres of the brain, but her emotions and womb as well. Not allowing woman to embrace all her parts pollutes her being. As both male and female forms we spend an inordinate amount of time aligned with linear, left brained thinking. Because woman is so crucial to human life, this imbalance and overuse of the left-brain, while denying that which comes from the right, cannot help but have a profound unbalancing effect on our society as a whole.

There is a difference between intellect and intelligence. Intelligence is the whole of knowledge intellect sources intelligence for its information. Left-brain thinking connects us to our mind, the place of intellectual mental processing. It is from our intellect that we associate with what has occurred in the past using that knowledge to prepare for what might happen in the future. From the left hemisphere we engage in survival practices of evaluating, judging, organizing, asserting; making no room for the birthing of a different experience. The right brain houses our intelligence; it is where we know without process, which is a connection to our heart space, not our minds. The right hemisphere of the brain is a place of creativity, intuition and wisdom where we are aware of the oneness of all life, while left brained thinking perceives separation. As humankind we are pulled by society to rely on the intellect to analyze what we see and feel, what we're told and what we've experienced; unaware that incorporating right brained processing will provide solutions from the heart space without the need to process mentally. The all-knowing Creative Intelligence is continuously recreating Itself anew providing answers to guide us to the newness needed in the world and in our lives. It recreates Itself into physical form to know Itself through that form. We call it The Creator. It calls Itself by your name, or by the name of a flower, a tree, an animal, an insect. As humankind It recreates Itself through woman. Woman is co-creator with Creative Intelligence to bring forth new human life. Conscious creation is the nature of feminine energy. Feminine energy resides in man and woman, but is exemplified as woman. The characteristics of feminine energy are predominant within the female form. It is a scientific fact that men tend to process in the left hemisphere of the brain where we are survival oriented, thinking logically and methodically. Females, on the other hand, have a propensity to process within both the left and right sides of the brain. The right hemisphere is where we are aware of the connection to life around us. It is where intuition, compassion and creativity exist. Woman's innate nature is creative. It is important in our evolution to align with that creative nature allowing its expression as your desires because we are always creating whether we are aware or not. We can create from alignment with our desires or we can create from alignment with our fears, our survival instinct.

Creation is an integral part of the human make-up. Conscious creation enables us to live the dreams that are shown us through the nudging of Creative Intelligence. When we become overwhelmed by that dream, we move into fear and stagnation, no longer aligned with our creative energy. The reason we become uncomfortable in the life that we are living is because something greater is calling. When we ignore that inner voice telling us which way to go, we don't receive the greater message. Creative Intelligence wants us to follow Its guidance. It will continue to call our attention to it. It is up to us, and our free will, to follow or to suffer. We tend to say that God punishes us for our transgressions when, actually, we are *always* being guided to right action. We exercise our free will to make decisions that are counterintuitive, causing ourselves anguish. When we continue to walk our path ignoring the inner voice we begin to suffer, inflicting punishment on ourselves. We are here on the planet continuously giving birth to newness. When we don't clearly hear what is being called forth a painful situation gets our attention. In our society we are so used to anesthetizing ourselves against any pain that we cause ourselves much more suffering than might be called for.

Conditioning and programming have led us to believe there is something to be gained from the outer world. We strive to become something we're made to accept as important rather than *thriving* by dipping into the wellspring of inner listening from which newness emerges. Society has taught us that our livelihood is determined by our ability to be assertive, competing for crumbs given by the powers that be. However, the life we desire--our true livelihood--is right in the center of our being. Sadly, we can't recognize it because we aren't connected to our feelings. Woman has been mimicked and criticized for her emotions and her intuition. We have, in fact, been taught to ignore them. We anesthetize ourselves so that we know no physical, emotional or mental pain. We never stop to realize, the Creator knew exactly what It was doing when it created human life--woman in particular-- with the ability to feel sensations including pain. It is our thoughts, feelings, and emotions that create the world in which we live. We have been seduced into thinking in alignment with a collective unconsciousness, which desires to control our behavior. We were not created to follow a path of fear. We are here to bring forth our desires and to be courageous enough to trust our inner knowing to guide the way to an expanded way of living. When we allow control from a world too small, we live in pain, which turns to suffering. It is the way of our economic system to profit from our elimination of pain and discomfort of all type. If we have a headache we take a pain reliever rather than feeling within recognizing the cause of the headache and alleviating the imbalance. We remove a cancer and never take time to look at its emotional cause so that we can recalibrate. Our programming encourages us to believe that someone else can "fix it" when there is actually nothing to be fixed. It is through asking "what is trying to emerge" when we become aware of our pain, physical or emotional, that we open up the communication line to that universal field of consciousness and can look deeper within our hearts to see from whence we are living and what we are projecting that is out picturing as our very life. If we are asking for a different result from what we are experiencing and continue to receive the same result, the universe is simply letting us know that we have not yet incorporated the steps that will move us to our desired way of living. When we then readjust and align with our ability to consciously create we have the opportunity to *play* in this adventure we call "Life" without need of feeling burdened or overwhelmed.

There is a clear calling which requires women to recognize our value as the embodiment of the Sacred. If woman does not embrace the significance of her gender the world suffers. The embrace of the essence of woman is our recalibration, our way of rebalancing, and a requirement for our society itself to come to a state of balance. When woman acknowledges and aligns with her true essence, it not only benefits those who walk on earth as woman, but humankind as a whole. Woman, you are the Muse who is expected to motivate others to inner awareness and connection. When we allow guidance from an inner knowing, we are revealing the Divine Sacred Feminine aspect. The energy being called forth is one which represents wholeness not competition, separation or compartmentalization. When woman, gives full expression to this Divine Sacred Feminine aspect, she provides medicine for us all. Woman, remember to remember, you are vital to the co-creation of life. Creativity lives in the right hemisphere of your brain, within your womb and in your emotional heart. Divine Feminine desires you to reacquaint yourself with your innateness to lead our men, children and women to an awareness of the oneness of all life. Divine Feminine has chosen you for the renewing of humankind. Fall in love with yourself!

Resurrecting the Muse

Express yourself creatively 15-20 minutes per day.

Everyone has some form of creative expression which causes you to become so absorbed in the act you lose track of time. When you come back to yourself you look with amazement at the creation and ask yourself, "did I really create that?"

If you are uncertain what that thing is for you, take a few moments to close your eyes and be still. Ask the universe to assist in your remembering.

Do you love to write, sing, decorate, draw, make jewelry?

Commit to spending time in creative expression (15 – 20 minutes per day) for the next 7 days. This is a commitment to you. Nothing is to stand in the way of this creative time.

On the 7th day also write in your journal what you have gained from aligning with your creative self.

My ability to get through my day greatly depends on the relationships that I have with other women. We all need that kind of community in our lives, but it is difficult to create if we are unable to sustain meaningful relationships with other women. Y'all know what I'm talking about. We have to be able to champion other women. We have to root for each other's successes and not delight in one another's failures.

Michelle Obama

CHAPTER NINE

Our United Power: Freedom

Woman: what if it is true that you chose to incarnate in feminine form at this precise time in history because the world needs your unique contribution for its perfect unfoldment? What if you can create a new way of living that serves you and heals the wounds of past and future generations simply by following your heart's true calling and allowing your presence to be seen and heard in your daily life? What if it means that letting go of the conditioning and programming that define "female" is the pathway to freedom from self-denial and self-hatred, not only for women, but our society at-large? There is an unconscious, prevailing thought in the universe; still, that woman is wrong, unworthy and simply not enough. Why? Because she is not a man! It is significant at this point in history that we are here in female form to free ourselves from imposed limitations which remain a driving force in woman's life. Perhaps it is through the pain and discomfort experienced that you discover the path to your greatness because "pain pushes until vision pulls." Countless times I sat in the audience of Agape International Spiritual Center and heard Rev. Michael Bernard Beckwith say those words. I understand their Truth. There is always something calling us to an expanded way of living. I know in my heart of hearts that women across the world desire to live from the fullness of their make-up. Women desire to no longer live from a disingenuous place within to suit others outside of themselves. There is a longing to live in active participation with a Higher calling. To do so we must listen within, follow the guidance that we hear and feel. Woman, the world needs your wisdom, your inspiration, your Truth.

To facilitate woman realizing and owning her truth, women must gather together with other women who understand the pain of disowning essential parts of self. They must reflect to each other the beauty of woman's innate nature; a reflection unseen in woman's everyday world. The most effective way for women to embody their truth is through seeing it mirrored by other women who know the pain and have found its remedy. Speaking inner truth provides women the opportunity to release external restraints and know freedom from attachment to the untruths that exist in unconsciousness. When you, Woman, are free our society will experience a greater sense of freedom. You will inspire others to their own personal release. Can you hear the voices of past generations crying out for freedom from the externally imposed restraints; suffering imposed on them simply because they had female body parts and woman's intuition? We carry their memories and their woundedness inside our cells. Their voices cry out from within. Their experiences impose restraints on our present existence even though we live in a greater appearance of freedom. There is far more passed through genetics than eye color and texture of hair. Women speak of downloading memories in childbirth, causing the emergent being to react to situations and personify unconscious beliefs not based on personal experience; instead reacting to inherited memories, feelings and ideas that exist in the collective unconsciousness. We have the opportunity to free womankind from domination, ridicule and invalidation through the true embrace of our hearts, no longer shackled by the beliefs that exist in a realm outside of our truth. We can release the wounds of past generations in gratitude for the path they paved by returning to our rightful place of honor. This return happens within. There's no need to force our presence and desire onto others. Nor is there benefit in making anyone wrong. The only requirement is to remember the stuff from which woman is made and own it within your being. You will then become a presence that attracts the respect and honor you deserve because you have aligned with it as the Truth of who and what you are. We will set free future generation of women because our children will no longer see evidence of a painful inner life, and only experience the honoring which results from our disallowed disrespect. We will attract the truth because we stand solid together in truth from this point in history forward.

It is important for women to come together in community to manifest their dreams. We must never dismiss the importance of coming together in community. Together women reflect to each other the perfection of woman the world so often strips away. We hold the mirror through which we can see ourselves completely, rightly, clearly. For so long, we have had the reflection of a collective belief system that does not honor our nature. It requests of us to behave differently from what our inner guidance tells us, to think within a particular mindset, to look outside of ourselves to determine who we are. By nature, women unite in community, talking, emoting, laughing and crying...together. When we speak our dreams to a world that does not embrace the true spirit of woman, we sometimes become confused. At times we experience a conflict that fundamentally does not make sense to us. Then we speak with other women and remember that all is well in our souls. We are reminded that there is no need to search for acceptance. We are seen and understood. We accept and love our unique selves.

We each have a unique gift that the world needs us to reveal, often discovered when we breathe into the pain and discomfort that gives way to the greater outcome, analogous to when a woman is in labor, birthing the new. All of humankind possesses these gifts, but it is woman who is the vessel through which Spirit incarnates. The womb is the representation of our uniqueness. Through woman's womb, dreams are dreamt and birthed into life. We, therefore, have the opportunity to let go of our connection to what anyone outside of self tells us we must do for the embrace of what we know of ourselves from within; no longer committing to the status quo. We align with a new way of being; a balanced existence which requires that we take our individual place of honor represented with integrity by our unique, essential selves. It is time to resurrect our inner muse, standing confidently knowing that you are a powerful force in the universe; so much so that you ignite that powerful presence within others.

The only way to get through the murkiness, the muck, the place where we live that does not serve us, is through waking up and becoming conscious. When we are awake no matter the situation; we know that life is good simply because we recognize the goodness; that we have value because we exist. Indeed, there is always something inside our beingness that is peaceful and honoring of self. There is something that reaches out to hold our hand and pull us up, guiding us through. The only way to accept its guidance, its love, and its peace is through our conscious awareness of its existence. To be aware we must stop the chatter within and let our self-importance be at rest, if only for a while. We will increase our awareness of *something*, which calls to our hearts to know our own lives more fully, to know the greatness for which each individual is intended. Divine Feminine is calling womankind into her embrace.

Within every person lives a secret desire for something more. I believe that secret desire does not reside simply in our hopeful imaginations. These desires are there so that we may connect with the intention for our lives and serve the purpose of allowing our unique contribution to come forth in our daily living. If we do not become overwhelmed by the feeling of actually having what feels out of reach or fear that we are incapable of manifesting our dreams, we can just sit with the feeling of having, *know* the certainty and allow it to become real. We can move dreams forth into reality if we do one thing each day to reach that desired dream. If that one thing today is only to daydream about it the dream is made real, at least for that time. When we feel the reality of our desires day after day we manifest our dreams a little each day. We anchor them on earth. What once felt impossible, we know can absolutely become a reality because "suddenly", we see it before our very eyes. We will witness woman discovering balance in her life and bringing balance to the planet because women are the givers of life. We carry sacred medicine. When we come together we dispense that medicine to one another. Together in the community of women we can feel united as family, anchored in our truth, enabled in our empowerment. Without such community, women are left attempting to find their own way with no nurturing support from like-minded souls. We live in a global community unlike our ancestors who lived in isolation. We are fully aware that we can touch those around the world with our compassion and our love in an instant. We can take this charge and lead our world into remembering that women united as a whole care for the hearts of us all, and thereby assist each other in protecting the balance of Life. Together women from all hues and cultures can unite to renew the individual soul which unifies the collective community of humankind. We begin the act of freeing us all by caring for the one life living inside each of us. When that connection feels solid within; love flows from it to womankind, to mankind, to the children, to the ancestors, our entire society and into the world. Women united, empowered, embodied by their inner muse understand that we are motivation and inspiration for each other and humankind as a whole with the ability to place a new belief about woman into the collective consciousness, shining the light of freedom into our world.

Resurrecting the Muse

Spend time over the next 7 days connecting with other women.

If someone comes to your mind call and talk with them with an open heart.

Schedule a gathering of women or participate in one that you know of.

Whenever you are in the community of other women remember to keep your heart open as well as your listening ear.

Be fully present to inspire and be inspired.

Make notes in your journal of the feelings provoked through these connections.

I am an endangered species
But I sing no victim's song
I am a woman I am an artist
And I know where my voice belongs
I know where my soul belongs
I know where I belong

DIANNE REEVES
"Endangered Species"

CHAPTER TEN

Resurrection

Upon awakening each morning, before her feet hit the floor, she smiles with peace inside her soul, excited for the privilege of living another day. In the quietude of the moment, she recounts the many things for which she is grateful. She is woman born; that in and of itself assists her in knowing, she holds a place of honor that breeds responsibility. She is eternally grateful for all that woman has endured -- the joy *and* the pain -- in stepping out of the shadow of her domicile to be an active participant in society at-large. She understands that her charge, at this point in history, is the recalibration of society. Woman is now to recognize the preconceived ideas about her character and let them dissipate, and with collective intention, encourage the remembrance of woman's worth, watch as womankind rises from the ashes reborn with a renewed zest for life, and takes her rightful place of nobility.

She is wired for intuitive processing and recognizes that when she fails to listen and follow her intuition's guidance, her body will indicate imbalance, as will the situations in her life. Her intuitive knowing will indicate to her where her strengths and weaknesses lay, her flaws, and where she excels. She will know when she is expressing from her heart or simply existing in fear, because she lives in appreciation of her uniqueness with awareness that her age, ethnicity, shape, style of dress, or how successful she is makes no difference to her degree of value. She understands that alignment with intuition is more important than ever in the multiple roles she plays and the many ways in which society depends on her guidance and direction. Her only goal in life is to bear witness to and deeply listen within each perfect moment, so that she may hear, and follow, guidance. She experiences inexplicable joy in realizing that she never needs to fear any outcome, because she knows, without doubt, that a greater *something* guides and directs her path. She needs only to follow what is shown. Her dependence on intuitive knowing relieves her stress and eases her life. Recognizing the importance of her role, she takes great pride in presenting herself to the world as open, receptive; one who listens and nurtures. Additionally, she understands the importance of taking time for her own replenishment because she offers so much to others while still valuing herself.

It is a dance...a delicate balance, which at times feels hard. Often she feels incapable of giving more, but for the common good, she remembers that it is the charge she takes because she is Woman. She is the one looked toward by men, children and other women to encourage a greater embrace of their own inner sanctum. There is nothing for her to do except let go of opinions, anxieties, fears, concerns, attachments and simply go for the ride. The only way to press go to get by the obstacles and what could feel burdensome is through meditation, dreaming, journaling and prayer...her sustenance. She watches the Light at the end of the tunnel come into clearer view.

The Muse in Greek mythology motivated and inspired art, song, meditation, memory, poetry, history, music, dance, astronomy, etc. As our world has evolved, the role of the Muse has expanded. There is a deep abiding sense of creativity within all of humankind. We are all artists in some way. We all at times have need for someone who understands and can bring us to a greater understanding of the occurrences in our lives. Everyone needs someone with whom they can be seen essentially, non-judgmentally, unconditionally and adoringly. It is not necessarily easy to live life from the heart in a world that constantly instigates grappling with fear. The medicine chest containing the remedies that promote a playful attitude and the understanding that life is simply an adventure is housed within the heart of a woman. That woman is called by many names; most importantly she is called by your name. You, Woman, are here on earth expected to remember that you are sacred, you intuit, inspire, motivate; you are the Muse with a directive to love. Every woman has within her a Muse asking for resurrection. Divine Feminine pours love into and from the portals of your heart. Open wide...breathe!

APPENDIX

In 2017 the #MeToo and #TimesUp movements catapulted to the forefront of global awareness by calling for the sharing of women's stories of sexual harassment and sexual violence. The World Health Organization has estimated that sexual violence affects one-third of all women worldwide. A 2017 poll by ABC News along with the *Washington Post* found that 54% of American women reported receiving "unwanted and inappropriate" sexual advances, with 95% saying that such behavior routinely goes unpunished. Long overdue polls and reports such as these expose the sexual abuse that has taken place and continues to occur in our global society, encouraging women to step forward and speak their truth.

In our postmodern era there has been a growing awareness that there is a certain "something"—frequently referred to as the Divine Feminine—asking for attention, acknowledgement, and acceptance. Her voice is reverberating throughout the world more powerfully than ever, giving Woman an opportunity to prove that there is safety and protection when coming out in numbers to confidently, freely speak about what she has experienced when declaring, "Me too."

Sexual abuse in all of its forms takes advantage of differing positions of power. Relating to positions of power is tied directly to one's perceptions based on cultural conditioning. As a woman seeks to become a valued and respected contributor to the society and everyday world in which she lives and moves, her understanding of power and who holds power over her can be aggressively implanted in her mind and embodied in her psyche. It is therefore incumbent upon Woman to take charge of educating herself on what constitutes authentic power versus false power. By doing so she equips herself to discern inappropriate verbal advances regardless of how innocent they appear to be, as well as overt sexual advances, thereby empowering herself to unequivocally reject such behaviors from individuals in a position to affect devastating damage in her life and affairs.

Fortunately, this is where the Divine Feminine steps in and splashes cold water in the face of false power by voicing that NOW is the time to carve new neural pathways in the collective consciousness of our global society. The success of the #MeToo and #TimesUp movements mandates that women must continue to fearlessly let their voices be resurrected and heard in all environments: the workplace, the home, schools, religious communities—any and every place where the need for a reality-shift is required.

Woman's perspective is urgently needed because encrypted within her is the ability to have an intuitive panoramic view—above and below, to the left and to the right, the inside-out of a given situation. Divine Feminine energy is the vehicle through which Woman tenderly feeds and nourishes those in her intimate circle, all those with whom she comes in contact, and the larger world. *But first she must nourish herself at the core of her own being.* This is accomplished, in part, by coming together with other women who can relate to both her pain and perspective, which supports her in genuinely, unapologetically experiencing love and compassion for herself, including those areas in which she has yet to evolve. Most importantly, it accelerates utilizing the tools which engage her intuitive knowing, for it is upon this knowing that the world can rely.

The Divine Masculine and Divine Feminine energies exist within the essence of Man and Woman. However, these energies do not exist in *equal quantities* within both genders. This underscores the importance of a woman's understanding that the Judeo-Christian tradition of spirituality and the principles and perspectives found in the metaphysical New Thought movement of the West emerged from men, heavily impacting the social structures and roles of women of their times and to this day. The truth is, men cannot speak for women, thus making the voice of Woman a vital presence in our world.

We have been led to believe that because there is only One Existence, one Life Force, that it operates the same in Woman and Man. However, our Creator Source has made itself very clear about the unique differences within its incarnated forms. Woman must understand this completely in order to carry the charge that is her unique calling, one which only she can fulfill. Man is essential to the fulfillment of the feminine aspect, just as Woman is essential to the fulfillment of the masculine aspect, and therein lies their equality. While Man can experience the fullness of the masculine, he cannot demonstrate the fullness of Divine Feminine because his cosmic wiring is different than that of Woman. This is why when he's focused on that football game and the baby cries, he actually does not hear the baby. Woman can multitask beyond human understanding and still hear that baby, no matter how faintly, in the background. Her emotions, along with right and left-brain processes, are wired to respond unlike a man's, which processes primarily through the left-brain.

As mentioned earlier, Woman has the innate ability to see life from a panoramic view. It is for this very reason that she MUST SPEAK from that perspective. If Woman's intact nature is not equally in the forefront of our ever-evolving world, something of major significance is missing.   Woman must know the importance of being Woman and contribute her voice, her presence, her energy to the world at-large, a world that yearns to receive her with open arms because she knows why she exists and who she is. Then never again will she feel less-than and walk in the shadows of those who cannot see how truly magnificent she is as she lives fully resurrected and expressed in her energetic wholeness.

#ResurrectYourMuse!

Notes

Notes

Notes

Made in the USA
San Bernardino, CA
17 April 2018